In Search of Myself—and Other Children

Eda J. LeShan

In Search of Myself
—and Other Children

M. Evans and Company, Inc. / New York, N. Y. 10017

M. Evans and Company titlés are distributed in
the United States by the J. B. Lippincott Company,
East Washington Square, Philadelphia, Pa. 19105;
and in Canada by McClelland & Stewart Ltd.,
25 Hollinger Road, Toronto M4B 3G2, Ontario

LIBRARY OF CONGRESS CATALOGING IN PUBLICATION DATA

LeShan, Eda J
  In search of myself—and other children.

  1. LeShan, Eda J. 2. Psychotherapy—Personal
narratives. 3. Child psychology. I. Title.
RC464.L46A34   155.4   75-38524
ISBN 0-87131-204-2

Design by Joel Schick

Manufactured in the United States of America
9 8 7 6 5 4 3 2 1

FOR FLORENCE,
Companion to My Inner Adventure

Prologue

In the early years of my psychotherapy, I had a recurring dream. A beautiful, ethereal young woman in a flowing chiffon gown of gray, which made her ghostlike, was gliding down the stairs of a brownstone house where I had actually lived when I was four to six years of age. I wanted desperately to touch her, but I knew that if I did she would disappear. In later associations to the dream it seemed to me that if I got too close—or if I even persisted in having the dream—I might become the young woman and then I would die. The theme of wanting to be close to her and the danger of dying repeated itself over and over again, for many years.

Ultimately it became clear to me that the dream had to do with a grandmother I had never seen, for whom I was named. In some mysterious way the dream belonged to my mother as much as to me; it was as if this was the dream my mother had never allowed herself to experience—her own longing for her mother and the terrible fears of dying associated with thoughts of her mother, who had died when my mother was four years old.

After more than thirty years of focusing my attention on the nature of childhood through formal education, personal experiences with children, and in discussions with parents, I finally feel ready to explore childhood through my own living of it and as I came to understand it in adulthood. The search has brought me back to that staircase and my dilemma—to touch or not to touch that ephemeral woman. Many years ago my mother gave me some faded, torn, yellowed pages of a diary her mother had kept when she was fourteen years old and traveling to Europe with her step-mother, sister and step-brother. I'd like to begin this book with some excerpts from that diary, written ninety years ago. I wonder what that Eda would have thought about being published, finally, by a grandchild she would never know; I hope the idea would have pleased her.

In any event, in 1899 a woman died at the age of 28. The fact of her life made mine a possibility; the fact of her death greatly influenced my character, my talents, my feelings about myself and about life in general. Before beginning the story of my growing up, I want to reach out my hand to the lady on the stairs—to greet my grandmother, in love, and without fear of dying. At long last I am able to relinquish the ghost without fear, knowing how deeply my grandmother still lives in me—all that I am, all that I still hope to be.

This book is therefore dedicated in loving memory to Eda Fleischer Schick,* who, even at the age of fourteen, could speak very well for herself.

May 31, 1885   Day One

After having bidden dear friends and family a hearty adieu, we started for Hoboken. . . . The sight alone of the large steamer which was to carry us so far away from dearly beloved ones, filled me with awe, and what Ernest † termed as "One short year," appeared at the moment an eternity to me. . . . I was already below, when a sudden jerk made me aware that we had already started on our long voyage. Mama stayed on board the deck until the last speck of dear papa was to be seen and then she joined me below. I noticed that her eyes were red, she said it was from straining to see the family, but I thought differently and tried to console her, but in vain.

* Her name was spelled "Ida," but the German pronunciation was "Eda." For the sake of clarity, I will use the phonetic spelling.
† An older brother.

Music was still being played on deck but it failed to make us gay. The view as we sailed out was a beautiful one. It was 5:30 P.M. and the sun, just sinking, made the green banks glimmer red and the water sparkle like silver. . . .

The first day on board was a bad one, there were but a few exceptions of the many passengers who did not find out the real meaning of sea-sickness. Thank God, I was not one of the sick, for what Mama would have done, had I fallen prey to the rocking, remains a riddle to me. . . . Carrie * cried that the ship should stop rocking as it made her dizzy. Eddie,† alone made sport of it all, and thought it such fun to be thrown from one side of the ship to the other and laughed heartily when he saw others in agony. . . . The bell ringing for supper, and sea-sickness having not as yet spoiled our appetite, we went below and partook of a good meal of meat, salad, potatoes, bread and lastly Tea and cake. It was 7 o'clock when we again ascended the deck. We watched the waves as they rolled, broke, and turned into foaming spray. Land was now a cloud in the distance and at nine o'clock nothing more of it was to be seen, so we went below, and after having lodged Carrie and Eddie in the bed (I might say berth) we tried to sleep, also, but Mama having already symptoms of seasickness, I stayed up with her until half past midnite and then I also fell into dreamland. . . .

* A four-year-old sister.
† A one-year-old step-brother.

Day Two

The night dragged along slowly and as the first gleam of daylight appeared we were already fixed to go on deck. Mama felt sea-sick still but not half as much as on the previous day. . . . The weather was beautiful and a small sail ship could be seen sailing far in the distance, as though it were sailing against the sky.

Mama, Eddie, and Carrie slept . . . in the afternoon and . . . I had finished my book called *The Children of the Abbey,* which was very interesting indeed. At 5 o'clock I joined in a game of croquet, and was even reluctant to stop when the dinner bell rang. The time between our supper and going to bed was spent talking of our home and those left behind us. It was not an unpleasant topic to talk about, but still it did not help to cheer us up, as we were more inclined to cry than to laugh. . . .

Day Three

Carrie and I went to watch the sailors on the rigging. High up on the mast's pole one could see sailors at work, speaking to companions below without getting dizzy, and I noticed that as they descended the rope ladder, that they often jumped 8 or 9 steps down, and never made a false step. Once while working high amidst the rigging a heavy rain descended upon them but they did not leave their work until the captain's whistle called them down.

Having eaten a ten o'clock lunch or Herring, mama and I suffered from an intense thirst, so I made a glass of lemonade, but as soon as mama tasted it she became sick and even I found that the lemonade had a peculiar taste. I afterward found out that the water bottles contained salty water. Many complaints were made the same day to the same effect and at last the provision master acknowledged his mistake. . . .

Day Five

. . . A week back from today I was in New York, a week from today I hope to be in Hamburg. . . . We have almost forgotten that it is summer for the weather we have experienced within the last few days has been so icy cold that we could not wrap blankets close enough about us, and a light rain drove us downstairs for the morning, so Carrie and I went to look at the Steamer.

We went to watch the machinery work and the constant up and down motions of the steel pistons seemed as though they were playing a sort of uninterrupted Jack in the Box. ... I asked one of the sailors, who told me that the Hull was constructed entirely of steel and that the Steamer had the width of 40 feet and a length of 375 feet. The Steamer has four decks, ... which form a most pleasant and unobstructive promenade. Directly above the promenade is the bridge where the Captain lives. There are ten lifeboats on board, so fastened that if one rope be cut the boats fall into the water immediately in case of danger. Yes, the Steamer is provided with every comfort, still there is not one single passenger who does not pine for land. We were told by the Captain that we might sight England on Tuesday, but if the days would only pass quicker that Tuesday would already be here is my most ardent wish.

Day Six

... The weather being fine, the promenade deck presented an animated scene. A Ball was improvised to the music of a hand organ, which a sailor played with untiring steadiness. ... How long the dancing would have continued I cannot tell, but the cry of "fish, fish," drew the attention of all, to the water, where hundreds of large fish were having a jumping match. It was very interesting to watch them, but our pleasure subsided when the Captain told us that it was the sign of an approaching storm. . . .

Eddie had become quite accustomed to the ship and runs around as unconcernedly as if he were at home, and not sailing on the briny deep. He has not forgotten his Ta Ta,* for how often he calls him, and the disappointed look on his face when he sees so many men but not the one he is looking for, makes us laugh heartily. It is now 5:30 P.M. That is just 2:00 P.M. in New York and I guess Papa is taking his usual Saturday afternoon nap, undisturbed by our prattling as usual, after which he is not lonesome for us? Or yes?

Day Seven

Sunday brought us cold and windy weather, the result of a storm during the night and we could not remain on deck in the morning. . . . The bell for meals seemed only a mockery to all, as not one seat was occupied at the table. When the second bell rang, Eddie must have thought it a signal that papa was coming, and cried "Ta Ta," examined

* "Papa."

-8-

every man's face, but in vain, he could not find the one he was looking for, so he began to cry. Mama felt very sick in the afternoon and laid herself in bed, . . . but the doctor would not allow her to remain below, as he said fresh air and exercise will go far to mitigate the sickness. It began to rain, so the doctor's advice could not be followed.

Day Nine

Tuesday morning brought me joy for I was sure of seeing land. The whole morning was spent in straining my eyes, in vain. Toward the afternoon, however, a cry of "The Lighthouse" brought me like a flash to the rear of the ship, where, after looking for 10 minutes I noticed that the supposed lighthouse was moving and it subsequently turned out to be a lightship. . . . But I was pacified by hearing that although we did not see land, the lightship was a sign that land was not distant. The prospect of soon sighting land almost rooted me to the place and even when the Supper bell rang I was very reluctant to leave it. But no land was to be seen. . . .

Day Ten

The bright, clear sky and the pleasant weather . . . seemed
to me rather prophetic of approaching joy. I cannot remember the time passing so slowly. . . . I stood at one side of the
ship so long until I could stand no longer, but hardly had
I seated myself when a joyous cry of "At last, At last,"
brought me back again like 2 fourty.* But Oh! Only to be
disappointed for nothing was to be seen on either side of
us but water. Many passengers gave up the hope of seeing
England and went below, but I would not stir. It was
5:00 P.M. exactly when I saw something in the distance
that appeared like a grey cloud. I could not speak my hopes
out immediately but waited to see if the cloud (like that
lighthouse) moved, but no, it stood on the same spot still,
so I cried out, Land, Land, but Oh! thank God, not to be
disappointed for after Telescopes had been looked through,
all were satisfied and a joyous cry of "Hurrah" was raised.
I was the Heroine of the afternoon for having sighted it
first.

* My grateful thanks to the staff of the Hyannis, Massachusetts, Library,
who joined me in the search for the roots of this colloquialism. To move
at "2:40" in 1885 meant to run as fast as the record for trotting races—
one mile in two minutes and forty seconds.

The joy we experienced on approaching nearer to it, I shall never forget. We could not have felt more pleasure had we found Captain Kidd's hidden treasure, than in sighting land. . . .

Why did the sight of the green banks make me jump for joy and wish for but 1 minute's romp on this soil? Was it because [for] 9 days we could see nothing but water, that made the sight of land so dear to us? . . . Our eyes were strained for we had watched the land like if we were watching a stage, while a theatre piece was being played.

'Tis true I had formed an entirely different idea of England, but what we saw was but a country hamlet. The green pastures and cows idly lounging upon them gave me the first impression of summer, for we had experienced unsummery weather all through our trip. I did not want to lose sight of this land, and so it was with a heavy heart that Carrie and I went to sleep.

The pages of this diary were yellowed and faded. It took days of great patience and eyestrain to decipher my grandmother's words. And yet I felt compelled to go on. In searching for the roots of myself it seemed essential to get in touch with this young woman and to savor her world at least briefly. I kept wondering what she would have made of our world and all that has happened since she took that ocean voyage. I feel such a kinship to her delight in adventure and the way she expresses herself—but when I think of the relative innocence of the times in which she lived, it is hard to imagine that we are related to each other.

One of the strongest links to the present, for me, is what she wrote about Eddie's crying for his papa and how they all laughed. I feel grateful to have belonged to a later generation, one in which I have played some part in our coming to a deeper understanding of the suffering of little children and the help they need.

I am partly rooted in my past and the way it has influenced my life, but I am also quite thoroughly a creature of my own time, and it is the balance between these two forces that I hope to explore in this book. Out of my childhood can I remember those things that can help me to be part of the shaping of the present and the future?

It is, of course, an impossible task; but so is anything else worth trying!

Chapter 1

Most people think I'm luckier than they are—or so it seems from the mail I get. "It's easy for *you* to write about changing and growing," one letter says, "you've already got everything!"

It's quite true. I had nicer parents and a happier childhood than most of the people I've known. I went to an excellent experimental school. I have been able to choose my work and have succeeded at it. My daughter and son-in-law are beautiful young people, my husband a handsome and brilliant man. I have a comfortable home in the midst of the excitement of Manhattan and another on Cape Cod for the necessary periodic vegetations of my soul. In spite of having lived through about five decades of the most terrible of times, I have rarely been immediately and personally affected by the depressions, wars, mass murders, strikes, demonstrations, poverty, unemployment, disastrous elections of terrible leaders, assassinations, atomic bombs, social change, unrest, and danger that have been coming at us faster than at any time in history. I have been safe and comfortable and have had a fascinating and rewarding life.

Half an hour ago I was sitting on the ground outside my home on the Cape, looking up at a young red maple, just coming to its full leafhood for the third summer of its life. It was so full of grace, so bursting with life. Near me on the ground were some blue pansies, and I sat there, weeping. We call the color of these pansies "Granjean blue." My mother's name was Jean, and when our daughter Wendy was about two years old, we tried to teach her to say, "Grandma Jean." Wendy made it one word, and that name stuck with two more grandchildren through the rest of my mother's life. Her favorite color was blue; it was her most flattering color and she wore blue a lot. Whenever we saw a purse or a scarf or china that was "Granjean blue" we were tempted to buy it for her, and she had quite a collection.

She died several years ago and her body was cremated. My husband and I had just bought this summer cottage, and my father and I agreed that my mother would have liked to be remembered by our planting a red maple in the front yard of this new home. Many years ago my parents had a house in Brewster, New York, and my mother had sat at her desk, writing, looking out at a maple she loved. Just after we moved in we had a tree-planting ceremony, surrounded by friends and family, but before that more formal dedication took place, my husband and I had carried her ashes here, and buried them at the base of the tree, the day it was delivered.

My husband was here several weeks ago, alone. He'd bought the pansies and planted them beneath the tree. When I arrived here, alone, to work on this book, I saw the pansies and knew why they were blue.

A few months ago, a younger sister of my mother's died. She'd been here to see the tree last summer. She was a character! An original. The funniest lady I ever knew; she could tell a story like no one else in the world; she had a repertoire of accents and a file of jokes for every occasion. She was a crazy lady, high spirited; always giving to others, unable to take from us, she had to give all the presents. If she loved you, you knew she would all but die for you. When my mother died, my aunt became my link to my mother, my past, much of my childhood. She died of a cerebral hemorrhage while telling some hilarious story to a rapt audience at the hairdresser's. I had not seen my mother's tree since my aunt's death—and suddenly, returning, there was such a flood of memory.

The thing is that being lucky doesn't make you happy all the time. In fact, I think that maybe it works the other way—at least it does for me. The longer I live, the more deeply I seem to feel. Because I have so much, and appreciate it, I seem to want more.

That thirst for "more, more" sometimes seems to make me preoccupied with death and dying. That may seem odd —even very neurotic, at first glance—but it makes a crazy kind of sense to me. Perhaps it is because in these last few years so many people I love have died, and the essence of their specialness seems more sharply defined as I remember them. Some months ago I mentioned to a friend that I felt loaded down by all the memories I now had to carry inside me. She said, "No, no, that's not how it is at all. Your life is *enlarged* by the gift of those memories—they make you much more than you otherwise could ever have been."

It's quite true. In some ways I feel closer to my mother now than ever before. I think I know more about who she really was, and she has surely had a great deal to do with the content of this book—as will, I hope, become clear in the next chapter. I see her exuberance, her life force, her humor and affection—how much she reached out to people who were hurting.

About a year ago a young man died. His name was Bob Kennedy, and people in Boston and Chicago knew him and loved him as a television talk-show host. After I'd written my first book, more than ten years ago, the very first invitation to appear on radio and television came from him. It was love at first sight—and included his wife and two adorable daughters on second sight. He was an insatiably curious man; he wanted to learn everything. As an interviewee you felt he was like a sponge soaking up everything you could tell him. He had enormous energy and vitality, and such a need to give.

Shortly after my second or third meeting with Bob, my husband went off to Europe and I didn't hear from him for more than a week. I was frantic. Then Bob called and wanted me to participate in a three-way telephone-radio interview with some child psychiatrist he was not too fond of. I told him I couldn't stay on the phone, because I was fervently hoping I'd hear from Larry. He was immediately sympathetic—I could feel the compassion rushing at me. He hung up, but called me back an hour later—he'd been in touch with the French Consulate in Boston! They were prepared to put on a full-scale search for Dr. LeShan! Fortunately, a cable came later that day; otherwise his wife, Bev, and I were sure Bob would have called Charles de Gaulle and ordered him in on the case! This young friend's death was a terrible blow, but my head is full of his essence—a passion for life, for missing *nothing,* for giving *everything.*

During my first year in college I played the role of "member of the wedding" to two classmates who fell in love. I was their best friend, suffering with them through the agonies they endured when both sets of parents tried every possible maneuver to separate them. They were both artists, although I don't think either of them knew it then, and the young man only came to understand that about himself toward the end of his life.

I found them fascinating. I was a provincial, protected, midlle-class girl who had never been away from home, except to camp. To me they seemed crazy and wild, although compared to today's young people they were pretty tame. I suppose they were an advance guard of hippiedom. They found an abandoned farmhouse and "furnished" it at the city dump. They eloped, with me as witness, and were married by a rural justice of the peace who happened to own a hardware store. The wedding took place surrounded by chicken wire, with chamber pots hanging over our heads! It was spring, and as we drove away from the college we passed a field of blue wild flowers. The young man stopped the car and ran into the field, making wedding bouquets for us to carry at the wedding.

In later years they lived through horrendous problems and a host of tragedies, but with it all there was a kind of spark of divine fire about both of them, and they enriched my world in so many ways. They helped me begin to learn about love, and they had a spontaneity and creativity that set a standard for me for many years.

One day, during the winter of our first meeting each other, we were driving together through a snowy woods. Again the young man stopped the car abruptly, and we made a snow maiden. I returned the next day to take pictures of her, and wrote the following composition for my English class:

March 1940
Somewhere deep in a woods where no one can find her stands a snow maiden. She is glistening whiteness in a vast green grove of hemlock. Three pairs of footsteps

lead to her. She is a secret known only to her creators and to the whispering understanding of the trees. Yesterday three gay, excited people, happy in their togetherness and in being alive in a snowy world, giggled and shouted like young animals as they teased the snow into becoming a playfellow. The world was small for the moment. Nothing but crisp white snow and tingling air to grow in. A grove of trees full of winter green drew their attention and having fallen in the snow and felt its friendliness, they wanted to use it for beauty. They built a snow maiden, high as a small tree, surrounded by nature's raw yet humble gifts she stands— alone today, but still part of the warm hands and glowing eyes that caressed her yesterday. She was started with laughter, built because of our need and she humbled us, for we had made something of ourselves and put greatness into it. In her arms is a child, made fast to her body by snow firmness and given movement by tree shadow. The eyes of the young woman reach to a small spot of sky between the treetops and as she clasps the child, she is yet holding it forth in rich giving. Her power fills the woods for she is part of the youth and the longing of her creators. Young eagerness formed her body and the unsaid, secret longings of young hearts have given her strength. She will not melt until the sun is really warm. Then, as spring persists, the sun will gently weld the child and the mother into one. No one walking through the woods will ever know that she lived to consecrate three lives. No one coming to that spot will hear the laughter, the sudden hush, or know the exquisite pain of being young and building greatly. But she cannot cease to be, for she was born of happy loving and expresses an eternity of truth.

Reading that today, thirty-five years later, I feel a little embarrassed by the emotion—and yet I feel so grateful for the fact that it was there, and real. My adventures with my young lovers were just beginning, and that time was filled with laughter and excitement and loving. How glad I am for it. The young man who gave life to this experience died in early middle age, a few years ago. His giggle, his aliveness, his pain—his love for me—seem to fill my being as I remember our being young together. His death did not diminish the feast of his life, in me.

When my aunt died, I was flooded by the special memories associated with her. When my daughter was in high school, a guidance counselor called to tell me that Wendy was playing hooky. It was a lousy school, and looking back I should have applauded her behavior, but I still had a lot of growing up to do then; I'd been such a model of perfect behavior as a child myself that I went to pieces completely. Where had I failed? How could we have such a false relationship? I howled in guilt and self-pity. My Aunt Anne gave it to me, sharp and clear. "Stop being such an ass," she told me on the phone. "Any child who doesn't play hooky in high school isn't normal. I stayed out a whole month once—and it might have been a lot longer if the principal hadn't called Grandma and offered her sympathy because I'd been 'out sick' so long!"

On another occasion, when I thought my marriage was over, she took charge of me. I'd let my husband go off to a meeting both of us were supposed to attend, rather than deal with our crisis. This time my aunt said, "You get the hell up to that meeting, you idiot!" In order to get me there, she met me, late at night, in one of the wildest downpours I can ever recall, at a Westchester train station, to drive me to the conference center. It seemed as if someone were throwing buckets of water at the windshield. I had no directions, and we had no idea how to get there. Every time we opened a window to ask, we both got drenched. Ultimately, anyone with the slightest degree of sanity had gone indoors, so there was no one to ask. We circled in the pitch dark for about two hours—but she wouldn't give up. We got to the right place at about midnight, and as she drove off she shouted, "Do me a favor—stay out of trouble, please! I never tell anyone other people's private business—not even Sam—but *you* figure out how I'm going to explain this little excursion!" With that she was gone, into the black and the pouring rain. And as I sit here, remembering, I am flooded with the aliveness of that woman—and the lovingness.

Recently, a friend of my mother's died. My mother had two friends whom she'd known since grade school. One was "Aunt Bea," the other "Aunt Lillie," who is now the only survivor of the threesome. I loved to be around when the three of them were reminiscing. Well into their seventies, they still giggled infectiously, their gestures those of fifteen-year-olds, as they described how they walked each other home from school each day. First they would walk my mother home, but since they could not bear to part, they would then all three walk Lillie home, and then all three proceed on to Beatrice's house. When Aunt Bea died, all I could think of was those three girls, gabbing, laughing, hugging, so full of high spirits. Aunt Bea was married and had two children, one a girl of my own age. I loved sleeping at their house overnight. Aunt Bea had a tinkly laugh, and she loved playing with us, with our dolls. One night, I woke up feeling very homesick and began to cry. I remember this pretty, sweet-smelling lady, coming to kiss me. She said she had some medicine for homesickness—you just chewed these little pellets. It worked perfectly. Looking back, I remember that they were really those little heart-shaped candies you get around Valentine's Day, but at the time she and I believed what we wanted to believe!

Lillie is the only one I have left, and we both acknowledge that much of what we experience together now has to do with memories. She was a dancer; she never married and she traveled all over the world. If I say to myself, "Lillie's coming!" I can feel a wild excitement, and my heart beats faster. I feel the muscles of my legs tense, as if I want to spring into action right now, race down the hallway as I once did, throw the door open and wrap myself around Aunt Lillie. She was our Peter Pan—forever young, forever adoring us—no matter what my brother or I ever did, we were perfect in her eyes, and with bursts of laughter and comic gestures she would entertain us endlessly with her adventures.

Death, memories of childhood—sometimes these tell us as much about the secret of life, about what it means to be fully human, as birth itself. I find a kind of "essence" coming to the surface when I think of people I love—and what it is, I think, is that they were all people who, in one way or another, said "Yes!" to life, no matter how much pain they might suffer. They were life enhancers, always greedy for more, and the more profoundly they experienced themselves, the more love they could give.

The "anti-lifers" tell us a great deal about the human condition, too. I know one or two people who, when they die, will literally not be mourned by anyone. Their lives have been tight and terrible, full of anger. I know a number of people who are my age and who have not been happy for one single day during their marriages, yet continue to live in quiet despair, totally unable to extricate themselves from their misery. I know people who have spent an entire adulthood moving in quiet succession from one horrendous psychosomatic disorder to another, and who cannot and will not ever face their own internal anguished cry for help.

A few days ago, at the intermission of a glorious opera performance, I overheard two women arguing. The venom, the fury, in their hushed voices was so palpable I could feel it brush against me. Apparently there had been some misunderstanding about where they were to meet, and one woman had finally gone into the first act still holding the other's ticket, instead of leaving it at the box office, so the second one missed the whole first act. I was sure they were sisters, because I cannot imagine such hostility expressed so openly outside of a family! One was furious because she'd waited, standing; the other because, being unavoidably detained, she'd been punished. They went around and around, blaming, accusing, and then they walked into the opera house for the second act, still fuming. As the lovely music began, I thought to myself, Here is the essence of what some people do with a whole lifetime; all that gorgeous music, and they are so crippled and tortured they can't even hear it.

It must start with self-hatred—early and deep and unbroken. Only people who give themselves nothing can be so unhappy, so angry and cruel.

One day I was walking through Central Park, feeling a sense of great exhilaration because it was toward the end of March and already I could see the first beginnings of buds on the trees. As I get older, each spring excites me more than the one before. The sun felt different—the air didn't bite—I could sense the rebirth, the joyous renewal, soon to come. An old man was sitting on a bench, yelling loudly at the middle-aged woman next to him. "I don't always look like this," he said.

Grimly she replied, "Your coat needs to be brushed. It looks terrible."

"She does it," he said, "but she didn't today."

Again, unlistening, tight-lipped, the woman added, 'It's dusty—it's awful."

I could not pull myself away, even though my mood was being infected, destroyed. It was obviously a father and daughter, discussing his housekeeper. He was defending, she was criticizing. There they were—with the possibility of something tender and nourishing between them. He was old; he'd soon be dead. Old hatreds, old guilts, cutting them off from each other. Did she feel guilty because she hadn't invited him into her home? Was he expressing his resentment by insisting somebody else could take better care of him? Were they both, perhaps, trying too hard to defend themselves against the grief and loss of a wife and a mother?

The day seemed colder, after all, less promising. I was reminded of a therapist who told me about one of his patients, who was probably going to die of a psychosomatic disease. Any time something good was remembered, any time they discussed ways in which the patient could become happier or more fulfilled, she would develop a nervous tic that she could not control; she would begin shaking her head from side to side. It was another way in which she was saying no to life.

Life haters don't only or always destroy themselves, of course; their self-destructiveness, their inability to affirm themselves, influences everyone around them. But there are even more insidious and dangerous forms of self-hatred, which lead people to murder, to enjoy warfare, to want to join with others to destroy masses of people who have somehow come to symbolize something in themselves that they find unendurable. The Klu Kluxer in his silly sheet invents for his own unconscious needs a black man who becomes a symbol of savage sexuality; because he cannot accept or endure his own primitive feelings, he strikes out against someone who has become the epitome of his own guilts and self-hatreds. The Nazi projects his own greed, his wish to make money and gain power, onto "all Jews" and is then able to turn the gas on and fire the ovens, in a compulsion to kill what he hates himself. The robber, the murderer, the assassin are all people absolutely consumed by self-hatred—desperate for punishment, caught between human needs they find unacceptable and rage against those they invest with what they conceive to be their own evil. The idiocy of capital punishment is that it provides the murderer with exactly what he is most desperate for— confirmation of his view of himself as monstrous and evil, a view he has had since the earliest years of his life.

We aren't born that way; what happens? Part of the clue lies in the fact that I have been exaggerating and over-simplifying outrageously! No one is ever *all* life enhancing or *all* life denying. Each of us is a mixture of both. Some of the people I've loved the most have poisoned their lives with petty grievances, laid waste some of their most crucial and necessary relationships through feuds having their roots in some unconscious past they refuse to examine. Some of the people who seem to me most crippled in their capacity to nurture their own lives are still able to offer affection, laughter, compassion to others. That's part of the mystery, the fascination. Isn't there some way to swing the balance, so that, most of the time, most people can struggle for becoming more alive than they are at any given time?

I wrote a number of autobiographies during my childhood—not from a narcissistic preoccupation, but because I went to a "progressive school" and had a "liberated professor" in college who encouraged introspection! The first one is dated 1934, when I was twelve. When it was finished and before I handed it in at school, I left it that night for my parents to read when they came home from a dinner party. Next morning I found a note from my father that said, "What makes me most happy is that you have so much zest for living. It would not surprise me if that were a quality you will be known for all your life—and there is nothing about which a father could be more proud."

I think my father's crystal ball was working well that day. By some mysterious combination of miracles, that quality has stuck. My childhood offered a lucky combination of circumstances. On the one hand, it was full of love and encouragement—which gave me that zest for life, a willingness to fight for what I wanted. On the other hand, there was also psychic trauma—old business in my mother's childhood, especially—that to some degree crippled me. It led me on a quest to search out causes, to want to solve the riddle of why I could be desperately unhappy, why I could do destructive things to myself. Because there was this ambiguous complexity, strength, and infirmity, I had both the will and the need to pursue, to go in quest of greater understanding of why human beings suffer and hate. I hope it is not self-delusion that now gives me a sense of having resolved some of my own conflicts, and in that process to have discovered some basic truths about human nature. The conclusion I've come to is this: It seems to me that there are three essential and vital stages in human growing, and that if the tasks that are appropriate and natural to each stage can be permitted as much opportunity for development as possible, it ought to lead to an increase in the numbers of life-enhancing people. Never all the same, never static or "finished," but having a not-to-be-denied hunger for self-actualization, not only for myself, but for every human being.

I hope that because I have had so much, it has given me the capacity to look more honestly—perhaps even courageously—at some of the agony of life, and to try very hard to see if I can figure out what it is that makes some people grow up greedy for life and some people grow up so crippled they never dare to really live.

I hate arbitrary age divisions, but to some degree they are really unavoidable. Assuming that these are only estimates —maybe even three or four years off in some cases, due to individual differences—roughly speaking, the first five years of life seem to me to be necessarily devoted to the quest, "Who am *I?*" the issue at hand being nothing less than what it means to be human. From six to twelve, roughly speaking, the major quest needs to be, "Who are *they?*" the issue at hand nothing less profound and essential than the problem of how does a human being see himself as special, follow his own needs, and still allow for the rights and needs of everyone else? Are these irreconcilable forces? Adolescence, roughly speaking, is, hopefully, a period when some of these issues begin to be resolved; when the fundamental question becomes "Who are *we?*" There must be a growing understanding that loving oneself enough to nurture one's own life inevitably leads to the maturing capacity to love others and to be loved by them.

One of the things I've learned from being married to a research scientist is that after you have struggled for years and years to figure something out and you finally find the answer, it always sounds too simple to be important or true! You break your back climbing through the thickets of your own ignorance and prejudices, you write it down and everyone says, "That's all you figured out? Well, everyone has always *known* that!"

If I seem to have suggested that the whole goal of growing up is learning how to love, well, that's how it is! The thought has occurred to quite a few people of considerable stature; my hope is to make it sound like such a simple process that everyone will be sure they figured it all out themselves!

In a profound and beautiful article in the *New Yorker* Magazine ("Prologue to Our Time," March 10, 1975) social scientist–philosopher Lewis Mumford warns us of the dangers we face in a technology gone wild, a humanity ignored:

... [A] onetime professorial colleague ... used to tell of a simple farmhand who had always battled against odds, raising a large family while barely able to keep his head above water. . . . yet he had never despaired. . . . Before he died, a visitor found him in a grievous condition, with an ailment that could no longer be fought off or grimly concealed. "Yes, my boy," he said, "My time has come. The feast of life will soon be over."

The feast of life! This phrase, uttered by a man who had faced more than his share of the burdens and miseries of life and seemed to have had too few of its rewards, is an affirmation that should confound a thousand nihilisms. . . . Far more lamentable is the kind of mental decomposition that takes place in those who have never consciously savored life's feast, for their unlived life takes its revenge, now sinking into docile acceptance of their prisonlike routine, now erupting in fantasies and acts of insensate violence. . . .

During most of the years of my adulthood, I had experienced a special kind of learning—beyond what I'd learned in school and in my various jobs. Starting in the late 1940s and continuing off and on, ever since, I have done a great deal of introspecting about my own life as a child through psychotherapy. I have worked with four different therapists. Except for the first, who was an orthodox psychoanalyst, all used an eclectic approach, taking what they considered to be the best ideas and techniques of many of the developing schools of psychotherapy.

Now, after all these years, I feel I have learned more about the inner world of childhood through this self-exploration than I could have learned from getting any number of doctoral degrees in child development, psychology, or psychiatry. It is unusual to persist so long, in examining one's own inner life, and I think it has now provided me with unique and important truths about the nature of childhood.

Why did I do it? I can't say for sure; I was never deeply neurotic—I could surely have survived without it. But there were many things I did not like about myself, and there were many normal problems and crises in my life; most of all, I seemed to have an enormous hunger for life—for living as fully as was possible.

In any event, it became my route for personal growth, and in recent months it has occurred to me that if I have anything left to say about childhood, I could do this best by using what is inside myself—what I have learned about being a child.

I will not be concerning myself with *techniques* of child raising in this book. I've done quite enough of that in the past and hope I've gone beyond that easy part! What I am after is to communicate a philosophy of life and its implications for human growth. If it makes sense, its application ought to follow quite naturally.

Life is so terribly short, so precious. What we need to do ourselves and help our children to learn is the necessity of risk; to use every minute of life we have for being all we can be, and helping those around us to do likewise. The feast, instead of the famine, of being alive and human. A friend wrote me recently, "The greatest calamity is not to have failed, but to have failed to try." Is there a way? I think there is. I have to try to find it. There must be a way for us to become less the victims of life and more the celebrants of it.

Chapter 2

It is absolutely impossible, no matter how excellent the circumstances of heredity and environment, for any human being to grow up without some emotional scarring. But that is not a message of doom; it is one of great hope. For once we understand that fact, we can try harder to minimize the hurts and maximize our sensitivities, without wallowing in guilt and false expectations. We might also begin to appreciate the fact that some of that scarring has helped to make us the interesting and unique people we are!

The problem and challenge of being human and growing up is that we are too young to have much sense during the period of time when we must, by nature's timetable, learn the most profound lessons. Imagine figuring out who you are and what it means to be a human person by the time you are five or six years old! *Imagine!* It boggles the mind. Well, that is what we are required to do, and it is a fulltime job. If we would only allow children to give themselves to that task wholeheartedly, we could surely minimize some psychological traumas, but I think I've covered that subject sufficiently elsewhere,* and my goal right now is to discuss *what happens* in the hope that that story will, in itself, give us the clues we need for what to do to enhance the human condition.

By the mere fact of having been conceived and born, we are already in trouble—and that's only the beginning! But let me explain this conclusion with the story of myself— for after many years of pain and struggle, I have concluded that my scarring has made me interesting!

I started that 1934 autobiography, mentioned in Chapter 1, with the following statement: "Up until about four years of age nothing of interest really happened."

Sigmund Freud has been making me pay for that ever since!

I had everything going for me—good genes and chromosomes, from a long line of bright, talented, hard-working, courageous ancestors; parents who were deeply in love with each other, wanted a child as much as one can ever be wanted, and who were two quite extraordinary human beings themselves.

* See note, page 74.

Shortly after my birth, my mother wrote a letter to my father:

> I'm really back home! And no one else is here right now, except Eda and myself! I like this—we are waiting for *you* . . . I feel weak and tired still, but stronger and a tiny bit surer of my ground each day. And each day I am happier and more consecrated to the great new work ahead of me, than which there is no more worthwhile pursuit. I could hug that baby so hard, couldn't you? She is *ours,* dear, and she makes our love richer and truer . . .

The following is an excerpt from another letter, written when I was about a year and a half old:

> . . . She was sweeter than ever today, so spirited and happy. We had such fun together before her bed-time and during her bath, Mary [the maid] was forced to ask, "Whatever would you do if you didn't have her any more?" (At which I still shudder).

My mother kept a Baby Book, with all the details of my development. The first entry is a poem she wrote about me:

> Baby, with your wistful eyes
> 'Gemmed with starry beaming,
> What is it that dormant lies
> Veiled beneath their dreaming?

Though my body yours has fed
Will our spirits ever meet
Or shall I hear your footsteps tread
Softly down another street?

You seemed so much our very own
To fashion and to mold,
But then you were quite young, you see—
Perhaps a whole month old.

While now I really know, my dear,
You've wings to seek swift flight;
I sometimes fear lest you may steal
Away, some starry night.

Nor do I bid you ever stay,
Sweet bird with wings to soar.
I only hope we'll keep you, dear,
A little, little, more . . .

A much later notation in the Baby Book says:

This was only the second time we'd walked to the
bridge, and Eda said, "Cooky!" immediately, remembering that we had stopped at a grocery on the way and
I'd given her a cooky. When we pass Renie's house she
recognizes it, and wants to go in. When Edith came
she said, "Ela, ope hat" and we finally understood that
she meant—Edith should take off [open] her hat and

stay! . . . She sees me with Argyrol dropper and hastily runs from kitchen, waving hand and saying "Bye, Bye." Says "Good girl," when she goes to the toilet. Pretends to read books, talking to herself. Calls me "Jean," roguishly and giggles at her own daring. Lillie taught her to "walk like a puppie dog," and if you mention Lillie's name she begins to walk on all fours.

In October 1927 my mother wrote a letter to my father on my first day at kindergarten:

Eda's First Day at Kindergarten!
It really was a Red Letter Day! Because of her excitement and my own feeling that she is indeed growing up. As I walked through the school holding her hand, I felt as if I was helping to enact the first scene of sending her out into the world. I wondered if the seeds we had planted in her little mind and heart would grow into flowers fragrant and fair—to add beauty wherever she went. And would there always, always be a feeling in her own heart and mind that she would want to keep very close to us and tell us of her thoughts —to want our help. It is easy enough to preach paving the way for weaning away from home—I do it myself —but there is surely a biological urge to hold on to one's young, to protect them, isn't there? Logically, I want her to go on. Emotionally, I shall have to control my simultaneous longing to hold on to her. She's really a fine little soldier. She cried a few times during the

afternoon, I was told later, but I'm sure that was due to excitement, tiredness and a failure on the teacher's part to tell her things she should have told her. But she tried hard to join with the other youngsters and to grasp what they were doing. She's a born "mixer" and she'll get there, I'm sure.

I do not think in all humility that we need to be ashamed of her. She is really a sweet, intelligent, sensible, lovable little thing, with plenty of initiative, a real sense of humor, a ready grasp of things, a curiosity about her surroundings, and she knows too about values —the worthwhileness of people and pursuits. I don't believe I ever loved her as much as I do right now! I love her so much that it just scares me and I feel as if I don't want to let her go to school at all, lest any germs get at her! . . .

It is hard for me to gain any emotional distance from these excerpts, but to the degree that I can I find myself, as a lifetime student and worker in the vineyards of child psychology, thinking, "What a wonderful beginning for a child! So much love and caring—how could it possibly turn out badly?" *It didn't!* All that feeling *was* communicated to me; I always felt deeply loved, and compared to the childhood of most children I was stupendously lucky. I think that is probably the reason I was able to look at the darker side of life as well. For this happy life was only half the story—and it is what I have learned about both halves that have given me a sense of what early childhood is all about.

I grew up to be a talented, successful, responsible woman. I have a capacity to give love, and have received more back than most people dare to hope for. My life has had a consistency and a security of professional satisfactions, family devotion, and very close ties of friendship. In addition, I suffered for most of my lifetime from terrible feelings of inferiority; I have spent a good deal of my time defending myself in neurotic and self-destructive ways from what I considered to be bad, impulsive, dangerous parts of myself. I married a man whom I have loved for more than thirty years, but who suffered severe emotional crippling in early childhood, and we have spent all of our years together trying desperately to heal our mutual wounds. I was not a very good mother; I was terrified and full of anger at first, and was so busy worrying that I lost half the joy I might have experienced. What saved all three of us was that despite our insufficiencies, my husband I never stopped trying to become more than we were; we were always in search of the best in ourselves, and our daughter grew up to understand that that struggle was the most important aspect of being human. At the age of twenty-five she wrote to us, "Whatever else this crazy family has done to itself we managed to generate a great deal of love for each other."

In any event, there was more to that happy baby than my mother wrote about. In the course of psychotherapy one begins to unravel the real ambiguities. The process becomes akin to the peeling of an onion; layer after layer peels away as you search for the deeper roots of behavior and feeling.

I think it might be helpful at this point to tell about my mother's early years, because the roots of the shadow side of my life began there.

When I reread that Baby Book about myself, I was shocked by an interesting omission on the first page, which was a listing of the grandparents and other relatives of the new baby. My mother had listed four grandparents, including her father and her stepmother. Her own mother, the Eda of my prologue and the author of that diary about the ocean voyage in 1885, was not listed at all, even though I was named after her. It seems to me now that in becoming a mother herself, my mother was unconsciously pushing away thoughts of her own experiences of being mothered; it was a source of too much pain.

I have a picture of my mother taken when she must have been about three years old. She is standing on a table, with her arms around her mother and father, who are standing on either side of her. She's adorable—with a pert and sassy and utterly delighted-with-life look about her.

I have another picture of her taken when she must have been five or six years old, sitting on her father's lap—really lying against him, passive, limp. The expression in her eyes will haunt me forever. She looks utterly broken—full of such enormous, palpable pain that it seems incredible it is the same child.

Is seems to me now, looking back across my life of more than half a century, that I have actually been spending a great deal of that time trying to solve the mystery of what is expressed in those two disparate pictures.

When my mother was four years old, her mother died suddenly. She was pregnant, and due to some illness a Caesarian was performed and she died from shock. The baby lived for a few hours only. When she died my grandmother was twenty-eight years old. From her letters and diaries and family reports, I gather she was merry and loving, wrote beautifully, had a charming sense of humor, and was madly in love with my grandfather and with her little daughter.

In a letter to her father, written in August 1896, when my mother was about two years old, she wrote:

> Today some men were playing music in the yard and the baby hollered, "Here is a penny!" and threw my pocketbook, which was on the table, out of the window. Luckily it fell on the fire escape! Ain't she good natured?

Two years later, my grandmother was dead. My mother was not told that her mother had died. She was told that her mother had gone away on a trip, that she'd been sick and needed a rest. My mother and grandfather went to live with my grandmother's family, and for about a year my mother was not told the true story. I also suspect that my grandfather tried not to show his grief in front of her—or if he sometimes broke down, he did not explain. That was not an unusual way of dealing with children in the early nineteen hundreds, and the proud stiff-upper-lip approach, "protecting" children from sad experiences, would have been characteristic of the intellectual and social atmosphere of my great-grandfather's home.*

About a year later, my mother was playing on the stoop of the brownstone where she lived. Two women were talking next door, and she heard one say to the other, "That's the little girl who was orphaned last year. Yes, very sad—her mother died—so young and pretty, too."

Today I can feel that child's pain so acutely that I have to remind myself it all happened more than twenty years before I was born. What happened was that without really knowing what I was doing, a good part of my quest for greater self-understanding and self-actualization was rooted in that experience of my mother's.

What, do we know now, happens to a four-year-old when a parent dies? We know that it is characteristic of all children, until perhaps six or seven or eight years of age, to believe that when bad things happen they are somehow responsible. In the milieu in which my mother was growing up, where good, decent people, in their wish to raise good,

---

* While I was working on this chapter, a great-aunt wrote me, "My mother [my great-grandmother] always blamed Hans [my grandfather] for his attitude—telling a four year old, 'Now we have no one.' "

She also sent me a diary belonging to my great-grandfather, in which he describes Eda's illness and death, the funeral, the memorial services in the home. One entry—"Many visitors, mourning services at house. At home all day. Children gay and jolly." A few days later he wrote, "Jeanette [my mother] crying with toothache all night."

All the grief, the visitors, the commotion—and my mother "gay and jolly"? How terrible; more than seventy-five years later, I shudder at the horror of her isolation and repression. But what was done was done with love, whether misinformed or not—and that was the bridge to survival.

decent children, talked a great deal about being "good" and being "bad," it was inevitable that the shock of desertion, as she surely saw it, must have been catastrophic. I know it permanently changed my mother's personality. I know it left her emotionally crippled all the days of her life. Nothing more terrible can possibly happen to a young child than to lose a parent, whom you adore and need desperately, and not to be told that it wasn't your fault and she hadn't wanted to leave you. That year of mystery, that lost opportunity to experience her grief openly, caused by good and loving people who just didn't know any better, and thought they were being protective, stunted my mother's potentialities and caused her unhappiness that she herself never fully understood or came to terms with.

I know this absolutely, because I "caught the trauma." In the process of searching, as an adult, through my own childhood, trying to find the reasons for periodic depressions, for feelings of self-hatred, for self-destructive compulsions, I came upon an intense inner sense of being in a black abyss of emptiness, filled only with terror. It became clear over the years, through many recurrences of such feelings, that in some way, quite unconsciously, because it was always there, deeply buried but crucial, my mother had communicated to me, probably in my infancy, that terrible wound she had suffered—her own black abyss when her mother disappeared.

Shortly after my mother died, my father wrote me:

. . . There came to my mind mother's excellence in

her work—and the heartaches, that in spite of her pioneering, her gifts, she was so often frightened of failing, being inadequate. It was such a senseless inferiority; what unnecessary nightmares. As time went on there was some intellectual acceptance of her worth and the folly of her anxieties, but emotionally there was no change . . .

On the surface of her life, little of it showed. Various relatives have told me that my mother had temper tantrums as a child, was very dependent on her father, and had a difficult time adjusting when he remarried. She must have been a stormy, complicated child—but there were so many positive elements in her life that she was able to surround that deep inner wound with very effective defenses and sublimations. Her father adored her, as did all her mother's relatives, and there were many. She lived in a strict and demanding household, but where children were loved and cared for well. She had inherited her mother's wit and gift for writing, and she surmounted the scar she hardly knew she had magnificently. When she died, several years ago, she was a greatly loved woman, who had made a tremendous contribution to other people's lives.

My mother was a pioneer in the field of parent education, and her relationships with the mothers in her child study groups was one of deep affection and humanity. She wrote two very good books about child raising.* She had hundreds

* *Life With Family* (New York: Appleton-Century-Croft, 1948) and *Do You Know Your Daughter?* (New York: Appleton-Century-Croft, 1944).

of friends—and none of these relationships was superficial. She wrote to friends all over the world, kept up with scores of relatives. She married the beautiful human being who is my father and had two great children—my brother and me! The good things in her life made her able to love others; the psychic trauma at four *made it impossible for her to ever truly love herself*. Despite all her gifts, she had the terrible feelings of inadequacy my father described in his note. Under the surface of her loving good spirits, she was haunted by that "terrible, awful little girl, who had been so bad, so unlovable, that it had made her mother sick and leave her."

I came to understand this not from my mother, but from the examination of my own life. I discovered from the beginning of psychotherapy that I was deeply preoccupied with a period in my own life when we lived with my maternal grandparents, when I was four to six years old. This was a brownstone on 153rd Street in New York (then considered the country suburbs, now part of Harlem). My father, mother, brother, and I lived on the top floor. On the first two floors lived my grandfather, my step-grandmother, and three children, then teen-agers, of my grandfather's second marriage. In the course of twenty years of on-again, off-again therapy, that brownstone house has appeared in my dreams more than any other place, and I discovered some strange irrationalities of childhood. I suppose that in some way my grandfather must have communicated to me that I was especially precious to him because I was named after his first wife. I suppose I must have had some dim notion that there had been someone he loved a lot by that name, and later dreams suggested that where most little girls fall in love with their fathers at four, in my case a good deal of that psychic energy attached itself to my grandfather. I discovered, again through dreams, that I had some sort of fantasy about being the reincarnation of my grandmother. I saw a beautiful young woman, a ghost, floating down the stairs in that house, and fantasied that somehow her presence meant that I might die, too. There was, obviously, from very early in my life, a strong sense of identification with the shadowy character of my grandmother, and an unusually intense relationship with my grandfather.

Another frequently recurring dream in the course of many years of psychotherapy was one involving a very young black child with an open, bleeding wound, with me somewhere in the background, either refusing or unable to do anything about it, and feeling a terrible sense of helpless frustration and guilt. My associations to the dream were that this child was the shadow side of myself—the unconscious part, the impulsive, irrational part—a side of myself that I was frightened of and wanted to reject and run away from. I knew that so long as I felt this way I would go on suffering from depressions, waves of self-hatred, self-destructive behavior, always concomitants of the denial of some part of oneself.

One day (in real life!) my husband and I went to a movie theater where they served coffee between the showings of the movie. A young black woman, who was serving, had her child with her. The little girl was about five years old, and dressed impeccably—stiff petticoat under pleated organdy, patent leather shoes, painstakingly braided and beribboned. She was adorable, but she had big, sad eyes that made me very uneasy. It was obvious that her mother was terribly concerned about the impression her child would make, and the slightest sign of restlessness or misbehavior brought a slap or a hushed threat, between gritted teeth. Whatever the reality of the relationship, what I reacted to was the feeling of an insecure mother expecting too much of a little child, and both of them trapped by too much anxiety about being approved of by others because they were so lacking in self-approval. It was the day after I'd been discussing my dream about the black child with my therapist, and I became increasingly restless, anxious, uncomfortable; I suddenly had an overwhelming need to touch that child, and to comfort her, but when I put out my hand to pat her, and said how pretty I thought she was, she became frightened and ran behind her mother. As we filed into the movie theater, I began to weep in the darkness. Finally I was able to connect with that part of myself—that hurt child whom I had never before been able to love and to care for. It was a turning point in my life, for this was the part of myself that was related to my mother's feelings of unworthiness, the fury of her loss, the terror of what she must have done to lose her mother—the terrified, lost child in herself she had hated too much to ever allow into consciousness, or to nurture. Ever since that episode in the theater, I have recurring images of taking that hurt child of my dream, cradling her in my arms and nursing her wounds. Ever since I have been able to mother my own life, at least most of the time.

At the very same time that my mother wanted me so much, and was so glad to have me, I was getting two sets of messages—that loving one and another one that I'm sure she was not consciously aware of at all—her enormous anxieties about mother-child relationships.

Sometimes in the course of very long-term psychotherapy, as one learns to be in touch with deeper and deeper parts of oneself, it is even possible to get back to feelings that seem to have occurred before one had any language at all. I have had such experiences in recent years, and they are, by their very nature, very difficult to put into words. What I have felt at such moments is a terror beyond language, of falling through black space, in which time does not exist. I have a sensation of hunger and rage, and without language or time perception, the feeling is that this is *always* and *forever*—that what I am feeling has no beginning and no end.

I feel certain that pregnancy and birth were far more frightening to my mother than she knew consciously, because of the complexities of her own childhood. My birth was long and difficult; I was born in June in the middle of a terrible heat wave. Nursing proved to be far from satisfactory, but in those days doctors were fearful of giving bottles in the heat of summer because of the dangers of bacteria in the milk, and as a result my mother and I struggled in torment through the summer. In recapturing those earliest months of life, the feeling is simply that nothing can possibly save me. But, like my mother, I was born to be a survivor, and raging against the terror, I made it through that first summer. What shocked me the most, however, in the reenactment, was that in some insane way I felt *guilty* for having survived. My own conclusion about this is that my mother had always felt guilty about her life force. Maybe it was that which had made her mother leave her; maybe she had been too noisy or naughty or funny or excitable; maybe all of those qualities of being intensely alive were what had made her the "bad girl" who was therefore deserted. Somewhere in my mother was that feeling, that to be a fighter-for-life was somehow dangerous, and crazy as it may seem to anyone who hasn't actually lived through such a psychological regression, I believe that in some wordless, paranormal way, perhaps, from my earliest days, my mother communicated to me her own sad and angry and frightened feelings about her unworthiness.

The miracle is, of course, that because she struggled so bravely to surmount her own emotional deprivation, I was able to grow up and fight against her darkness; I relinquished that self-hatred by knowing it—and I could not have gone through that often terrifying struggle unless I had also felt worthwhile and lovable. That is, for me, the miracle of life; that with each new generation there is a chance to undo some of the pain—to allow for more self-acceptance. Despite the ways in which I failed in the early years of motherhood, I was well along the trail of my own self-understanding, and at twenty-five my daughter has more insight, more self-understanding, more compassion than I had at forty.

I was especially interested in finding that letter about my first day in kindergarten, because my later recollections of that day are very different. When my mother left me, I was sure I'd never see her again. By that time my mother's unconscious fears of a similar (and actual) separation were already deeply part of me. I would experience waves of such terror into my forties—the empty abyss, the mothering suddenly gone.

The fascinating thing about being able to examine one's past through external observations as well as internal ruminations is that every truth is only a half-truth! My mother was quite right when she predicted I'd be "a born mixer." I'm sure it even looked that way when I was very young. But my inner recollectons of all my years of growing up, into early adulthood, are that I *felt* unpopular, shy, ugly, a loser, and an outsider. The same pattern as my mother: all the attributes for feeling so fully alive, so glad to be who we were, with the gifts we had—and always that background music of feelings of unworthiness.

It was also true that I eventually adjusted well to experiences away from home. But never without inordinate anxiety about desertion. Some time later, during that year of kindergarten, my Uncle Edward took me to school. It was some sort of holiday, and I wasn't sure the school would be open. He left me a few feet from the school door and turned to go back home; he was in high school or college, and didn't have any school that day. I tried to open the school door and then panicked. I was sure it was locked and that I would be deserted and alone. I ran screaming down the street trying to catch up with my uncle, and until I did, several blocks later, I felt absolute terror. He walked with me back to the school and opened the door for me—school was, indeed, in session.

A recurring dream in adulthood was that my father took me to the front steps of my elementary school and said good-bye—and then I discovered that I was naked. I would be overwhelmed with feelings of panic and loss. In actuality I was pretty happy at school—it was one of the best progressive schools of that period, and in general a far more loving environment than most children experience in school. And yet I felt so nakedly vulnerable, so afraid of desertion. Similarly, it took me long periods of time to adjust to being away from home, at camp—even when I went to college.

One of the most helpful insights that have come to us in the revolution in psychology is that *feelings that are most deeply repressed by a parent can sometimes have more influence on the life of a child than feelings that are close to the surface of consciousness.* In spite of the genuine feelings of love and joy expressed by my mother, I was equally well tuned in to her feelings of deprivation and desertion and her typically childlike assumption that in some awful way she had been responsible for her mother's death.

Why bother to write all this—to tell this story? The benefits of catharsis and insight were gained long since. I suppose I have wanted to add it as another dimension to what I have written in previous books about the nature of childhood; I see it as the most authentic part of my own "research," a final crystallization of what I believe to be true about children.

I see nothing accidental about the fact that my first career was as a nursery school teacher. As matter of fact, I started that career at the age of twelve! But long before that I had already assumed the responsibilities of motherhood; by the time I was four or five I had a dozen dolls, each of whom had a specific name, each cared for diligently every day. No tossing them on a shelf or into a toy box for me, but days of "slaving away" over their imaginary meals and diapers and naps. Each night when my father came home from work, I would report on their behavior and well-being. I played with dolls until I was about ten or eleven, giving them up reluctantly when people laughed at me wheeling a doll carriage on the street, but the degree of my emotional involvement was so intense that even in college the walls of my room were plastered with baby pictures at a time when I ought to have been preoccupied with very different human relationships.

By the time I was twelve it was clear that I was "a natural" with little kids. I was living in a summer colony where there was a day camp, and a marvelous young woman, who was camp counselor to the three-year-olds and who later became the director of an experimental school in California, asked me if I'd like to be her part-time assistant. Later that summer she asked me what I wanted to be when I grew up, and I told her I wanted to be an actress. She suggested I give serious consideration to working with children.

Somehow that discussion stuck with me all through the years, and I knew I had come to the ultimate resolution of these conflicting choices when I had my own television program on child raising!

Because of the love of my parents and the good feelings they helped me to develop about myself as worthwhile and lovable, I think I was strong enough to always keep some channel of communication open with the painful parts of my early experiences—I was not so seriously damaged that I needed to repress them altogether—and this combination was enormously effective in working with children. From the beginning, I seemed to identify with their feelings, understand their needs. High school courses in child psychology, college, graduate school, all seemed merely to confirm what I already "knew" (sensed) long before. I suppose that becoming a nursery school teacher was a kind of undoing; I knew how scared—deserted, even—a child could feel, and I was able to come to terms with my own early anxieties by being the strong adult who could help; I was really comforting the child inside myself.

Some years ago, when I was a consultant to a nursery school (which involved in-service training of teachers, parent conferences, and discussion groups), I found myself spending a great deal of time explaining "separation anxiety." It is my not-at-all humble opinion that I am one of the world's greatest experts on this subject! I used to love to demonstrate to the new teachers how to handle the weeping child—never by saying "you'll be fine," but always confronting the real feelings of the child quite directly; "I know how scared you are, and angry at Mommy for leaving you here. It's good to cry—let me hold you and comfort you." It has become eminently clear to me that my "success" in reassuring was that *I* was that child.

As I began to explore my own early years I found that they helped me to crystallize the most essential aspects of the process of growing up, and it is that distillation which I think may be helpful to other people in learning more about themselves or in helping them as parents or teachers of young children.

What was confirmed most profoundly by my inner adventure was that by the time a child is five or six years old, he has developed a relatively clear and consistent self-image. This self-appraisal is very powerful and very resilient because its original impact occurs at a time when a child has the least information about the world, the least experience, the least language facility for communication and is most vulnerable—as vulnerable as it is ever possible to be.

This self-image is full of primitive distortions that are at least to some degree unavoidable—and because they *always* interfere with later perceptions of oneself and other people, they need to be examined consciously from time to time in adulthood.

For example, right now, this minute, say to yourself, "What was I like when I was four years old?" Write a list of characteristics—of how you *felt* about yourself. I've repeated this exercise with many groups of parents, and these are the words that crop up on such lists most frequently:

"Too shy; too fat; funny-looking; dumb; too fresh; scared of stupid things; clumsy; too restless; bad."

It is desperately important that we understand how this happens, so that we can help ourselves by reevaluating these childish and incorrect observations, as well as do what we can to minimize such distortions in our children, for if we have learned anything at all with certainty, it is that we make ourselves and the world around us full of misery when we carry the burden of poor self-perceptions into adulthood.

It seems to me that probably one of the central reasons that human history is so bloody and so awful is that no society has yet been able to solve this problem, that a child's earliest ideas about himself and other human beings are gained during the earliest years of life when he is least equipped to make reasonable judgments!

It always seemed to me that infants were able to sense parental feelings long before language was available for communication. My explanation for this (and that of many experts) was that babies took such cues from the body language of their parents—sensing tension, anxiety in parental movements, heartbeat, and so on. I'm sure that's true, but I now believe there's more to this "sixth sense." For many years my husband has been researching the field of parapsychology, and it now seems to me that all human beings are born with two ways of learning about the world —through the senses and the way of the clairvoyant, in which another kind of consciousness is operating. This is especially true before language begins; in fact, my feeling is that this natural attribute, which is an important resource for human fulfillment, tends to be lost when language begins. The more "civilized" a culture—the more the emphasis is on cognitive learning—the greater the loss of this initial ability—and the more serious the crippling of "human nature."

However, the implications of this are best left to my husband, Lawrence LeShan, the family researcher. What I am most concerned with is that we *do* get mixed messages long before language, and that because we have no experience with the limitations of time and space, everything we feel in infancy is *always*. That explains the terror—and it tells us a good deal about the meaning of infant crying. When a child is hungry or exhausted or wet or lonely, these feelings fill the whole universe; they have no beginning and no end. You and your pain are all there are, or will ever be.

It is a source of pain to me that I didn't really come to understand this feeling until my daughter was grown up. When it would have been helpful—appropriate—to understand, I didn't. Like most other parents and pediatricians, I had this insane idea that if I picked her up every time she cried, she'd go on doing that for the rest of her life! To the degree that I could, if she were a baby now, I would, first of all, have one of those marvelous carrying sacks that weren't available twenty-five years ago. When she was unhappy, I'd "papoose" her, and if she cried really hard at night, I'd take her into my bed. The terror is palpable and real to me now; *she had no way of knowing if her discom-*

fort or her fear would ever go away. There is no possible
way for any number of adults to meet all the needs of a
child, and I wouldn't feel guilty about the times when I
failed—but I sure as hell would *hold* and *comfort* in a way
of which I was totally incapable then.

What happens is that most of us never recover those
earliest memories; we can't bear to—they are too terrifying.
Then we have a child of our own, and it is like being forced
to remember something you cannot bear to remember—so
you remove yourself to a safe distance. You like ideas about
"dangerous habits" and "crying is good for the lungs." They
offer an avenue of escape, to keep your own infancy terrors
away.

I wonder what kind of a grandmother I will be. It will
be a real test of what I have lived through. I am no longer
scared of what a baby is feeling; I can share it now. I
could, I think, *join* a baby in its feelings, and this would
make me less tense and frightened and more able to give
comfort.

This period of total confusion and crazy perceptions gives
the young child his or her first feelings about "who am I?"
And because thinking is so primitive, it is hard to imagine
any child coming unscathed into consciousness without
some very deep sense of being bad—a wordless feeling of,
"If I were good, someone would make me comfortable all
the time; I must be bad because I'm making somebody
angry and upset." But these are feelings *without language,*
which makes them far more agonizing and overwhelming.

If I were a young mother today, nobody could possibly

convince me that picking up a crying child could help to form "bad habits." A child outgrows the nonverbal period; he learns about time, he reaches a point where he can express his feelings in words. Then the wordless terror begins to abate, and being left alone is not to fall endlessly into a black abyss of terror. Meanwhile, to the degree that I could, I would offer body comfort, and I think I would find it far less exhausting and demanding because now I would be allowing myself to identify fully with a baby's feelings.

During infancy, the terror is so great that we repress it as fast as we possibly can. Getting back in touch with those feelings, through psychotherapy, as an adult isn't easy, and there is plenty of anxiety and pain—but it is totally different. Now I was an adult; I could understand and control it. I would *not* suffer endlessly; I would not die. Now I know about time and space; now I can take care of myself. But *knowing* about these earliest feelings has been enormously helpful.

I learned, for example, why the young child clings to familiar objects. They help him locate himself in that endless space and time. During the period when I was reexperiencing some of the earliest feelings, my husband and I were moving—just from one apartment to another, same building, same furniture. The first few days I went to pieces. Nothing looked familiar in the new setting; I felt lost in space. There were vaguely familiar objects, but they appeared to me to be part of some sort of terrible chaos—

utterly strange. It was home but not home. I couldn't seem to distinguish what was "real." I felt frantic.

During the early years of life, when perceptions of "reality" are primitive and distorted, the same objects in a new location become frightening and unreal. To some degree this continues in children for many years. Feelings of confusion about time and space are, undoubtedly, related to the way a child clings to his special blanket or a teddy bear. It accounts for the emotional disturbance in young children when a family does move from one home to another, or when we take children to strange new places—a friend's house, a store, a nursery school. I recall one mother telling me about a three-year-old who was inconsolable after a move—couldn't sleep, cried, had nightmares when she finally did fall asleep, and so on. This went on for several weeks, although the parents kept pointing out that all the toys and the furniture in her room were from the old house. About three weeks later they wallpapered her room in the same paper they'd had before. They had liked it, and couldn't find anything they liked better. "It was a miracle!" the mother told me. "Stephanie took one look at that wallpaper, sighed deeply, put her thumb in her mouth, and went to sleep for ten hours!"

Several years ago I wrote an article for *Woman's Day* Magazine* about something that had happened to me a few days after my mother's death, when I was alone in a hotel in San Francisco. I had bought a toy, a stuffed baby seal, to give to a niece, and in the middle of the night, weep-

* August 1973.

ing, I had taken it into bed with me, rocking back and forth, singing a lullaby my mother used to sing to me. The next day I got a second seal for myself and brought it back to New York, having discovered that at fifty I was not too old for such comforting! After the article appeared, I received a package from a reader in California. She had sent me a homemade "Winnie the Pooh," made out of brown corduroy; he was enchanting. Her note said, "I recall reading that you have an apartment in New York and a summer home in Massachusetts, and I didn't want you to be without a stuffed animal in your second home." There have been any number of cold, lonely nights on the Cape, when I have sent myself into solitary confinement in order to write, when I have wrapped myself around Pooh and silently thanked that beautiful lady who sent him! Such comforts are the secondary gains of therapy that puts one in touch with one's deepest needs.

I received hundreds of letters about this particular article —all of them acknowledging similar kinds of experiences and feelings. One in particular touched me deeply. A woman wrote that she had returned alone to her parents' home in the Midwest. Both parents had died over a short period of time, and she, the only child, had to sell the house and its contents. It was a very painful time for her, but she was staying with an aunt who lived nearby during her stay, rather than be alone in the house. One day a blizzard started, and by the time she realized what was happening, it was impossible to leave. She had no choice but to spend the night alone. She said, "The one thing I had not been able to do was go through a trunk of my old toys in the basement. As the storm became worse and my isolation more painful, I remembered your article about the seal, and I went down and opened the trunk. I found my favorite doll, took her up to bed with me, and began to weep for my loss and my memories. For the first time I realized I could be alone and comfort myself."

Of all the characteristics of early childhood, none is more significant than self-reference; whatever happens, the child feels responsible. It is a kind of primitive thinking that seems to be inevitable when you have not yet been able to sort things out; to know where you begin and end; to understand real causes and effects; to see yourself not as the center of the universe but a part of many interrelating people and experiences. It is the "it's all my fault" syndrome. My mother, at four, did not understand illness and death. She had no way of understanding that grownups could be ignorant of children's needs and could be mistaken in their ideas about what it means to be loving and protective. All she could experience was that suddenly her mother disappeared. Her only possible interpretation (within the limitations of her perceptions) was that she must have done something bad.

I, in turn, had no way of understanding my mother's unconscious anxieties about mothering, her feelings of unworthiness. If she was tense and anxious, it had to be something *I* was doing wrong. All the events that can be understood, later on, as part of a totality of experiences over which we did not really have any control are perceived in the first years of life as forms of personal depravity. We don't understand that we are at the mercy of our impulses and fantasies merely because we are little. We don't understand that because we have no experience, no judgment, we take all our cues from those adults around us whom, in our helplessness, we need so desperately.

The first impressions you have of yourself come from other people. What you think about yourself depends on what they think of you, and the messages you get tend to be confusing, contradictory, and ambiguous—even more so after you begin to understand words. Somebody says, "What a beautiful baby"; somebody else says, "Too bad she's got Charlie's nose." Some days a nice lady called a mommy tells you you're "a good, sweet child"; even an hour later, she can be screaming that you are "a bad, bad girl." How is this possible?

As children grow, the "good" parts of being human fall into place very easily. People love you like crazy when you kiss and hug, when you eat your vegetables, when you give another child a toy, when you go right to sleep. The same people can make you feel absolutely terrible. If you bite or scratch, or grab or hit, or cry at night or feel scared or shy, they tell you that you are being bad. If you get angry, you're bad; if you touch your face and point to your eyes and nose and mouth, you're cute; if you touch your penis or vagina, you're being very bad. If you take some pot covers and bang them together, one day Daddy will laugh; the next day he'll scream, *"Stop that noise!"* If you take the blocks off the shelf and pile one on top of the other, somebody beams and says, "That's wonderful!" If you pull the books off the shelves, somebody will probably hit your behind and say, "No! Bad!"

Sometimes terrible things happen. A mother disappears; you don't know if you will ever see her again—and when she reappears you have no idea how long she's been away, or what might happen next time. Did she go because you were bad? Will she stay if you are good? Or you hear a lot of fighting and yelling, and you begin to cry, and then, suddenly, a daddy disappears and you never see him again. Or a mommy goes to bed and everybody tells you to be very quiet, but you are scared and you yell a lot, and then she's gone and she never comes back. Your poor little brain is so unfinished that you can only assume that the daddy went away because you bothered him or the mommy went away because you bothered her.

All young children think in this kind of self-reference. They feel that they are the center of all things and the cause of all effects. This makes them responsible for fights, death, divorce, illness, anger, impatience—all the awful things that can happen.

Most of all, you are in a lot of trouble if *you* get angry, or do anything mean to anyone else. You're only three years old, for God's sake, and already there's this damned baby living in the house; if you hit it or bite it or take its toys, everybody hates you and they hit you or yell a lot. Or you don't want to sit on Grandma's lap and they say you're "not nice." Or you take a wagon away from Sarah and they say, "You're a bad girl," or you hit that terrible boy from next door, and they tell you that's a bad, bad thing to do —and then they hit *you*. Life is a puzzlement, all right! It's clear that good people are gentle, loving, kind all the time. If a grownup gets angry, it's because *you* are bad. But only rotten, mean kids like yourself get angry and do bad things, without any good reason.

What's important about sex in the early years is the same thing that makes anger so important; it's a subject fraught with danger because people give you such mixed-up signals about it. For reasons totally beyond a young child's understanding, some parts of the body seem to be "nice" and some "dirty." Some parts of the body have names that everybody wants you to learn; other parts—you must *never say* the words out loud, in front of certain relatives, in an elevator, on a bus, or in a store. It's perfectly okay to do some pleasurable things—smell a flower, roll on the grass, suck on a lollypop, but if you give yourself other pleasurable sensations, by touching yourself, people tell you to stop it, or they wash your hands, or they get angry—or some even tell you your fingers will fall off, or that God is watching and what you are doing is sinful. It *seems* so natural—but obviously you must be a terrible person if that's how grownups act.

There seem, on careful observation, to be two basic kinds of human beings—girls and boys. Some people think that's funny—it causes them to giggle. Some people just never talk about it at all. There seem to be some arbitrary rules about what boys and girls may or may not do, and these seem utterly absurd most of the time. Daddy doesn't like it if you want a doll if you are a boy; Mommy doesn't like it if you never want to wear a dress and you're a girl. Why? And if two girls hug and kiss, that's fine, but if two boys hug and kiss, that's bad, and if a boy and a girl hug and kiss, people joke about it until you feel shy. *Why?*

Sex and anger are the two facets of being human that we handle most ineptly, stupidly, cruelly, and *that* is why they've seemed to have such monumental importance in the early years—and why so many of our social problems, throughout human history, relate to these issues. We have tended to ignore the distortions of early judgments. If a kid was lucky and the people around him loved him a lot, he was able to survive all of this without too much psychic damage but certainly some, enough to possibly give him migraine headaches, or make him join a gang stealing other people's belongings, or never be quite able to love anybody that loved him back—all indications of poor feelings about oneself.

If you were very unlucky, there were whippings instead of spankings, and horrendous cruelties—a clear indication that you were depraved, worthless, so full of sin you'd burn eternally in hell. (Every ex-convict I've discussed this with had such feelings.*)

Such disasters are avoidable. While the nature of human nature will, I hope, always remain mysterious and unpredictable, and each of us will grow up with our own beautiful eccentricities and gifts, *it is not necessary for any human child to grow up hating himself*. We need to understand

* In discusions at the Fortune Society.

this so we can examine the ways in which we torture ourselves, and we surely need to understand it if we want to be parents.

We have to learn to deal with these distortions. We can make every "mistake" in the book, some of the time, and still help a child come out all right. First of all, we need to understand the terror of having no limits on time or space, so that when an infant cries we are not afraid to repeatedly give comfort. Later on, when a child understands "a minute" and "tomorrow" and "this room" and "the park," we can begin to impose regulations and expect children to accept and endure frustrations and temporary discomfort. Crying for what you want, crying because you are lonely, is no more habit forming than feeling without language; both are temporary conditions of growing.

Just as important, we need to make it clear, as soon as language becomes reasonably well established, that no child is bad or good—only human—and that thoughts and words can *never* make bad things happen. All human beings are saints and sinners, angels and devils. The younger you are, the harder it is to control uncivilized behavior; that's why there are adults around, to teach, to help you gain control, so that you won't do anything to other people you wouldn't want them to do to you. It's not a question of good or bad; it's being human and little. Furthermore, thinking angry thoughts is normal and not at all dangerous; neither is saying angry thoughts, only *doing* things that hurt. Because language is new and thoughts are still quite primitive, children at first assume that if you think, "I'd like to kill that monster who is yelling at me!" Daddy will suddenly drop dead on the floor. We have to clarify the difference between thinking in words and doing in action.

Being shy, afraid of the dark, jealous, selfish, inclined to bite and hit, inclined to take what you want when you want it are all normal parts of being a person and of growing up. With a little bit of luck and a lot of help, some of the things that get in the way of feeling good about yourself and getting along with others will change for the better—but what is so marvelous is that each of us will still be different from everybody else in the world.

If we could go back to our own childhoods and reassess how we felt about ourselves; if we could reorder the distortions, how much more fulfilling and creative our lives might be! And if we are young parents and can do this part of it right, none of the details (the right month for weaning or toilet training, or starting nursery school, which baby foods, which diapers, etc., etc.) will really matter very much at all.

Our first self-perceptions reflect how our parents feel about themselves, and this inevitably includes their ambitions and goals for us. One of the things I learned from my own explorations is that love itself can sometimes make it harder to grow up to be oneself. In my case, my parents' love for each other and for me, their own talents and ambitions, tended to produce in me a rhythm of life that was not really my own.

I go stark, raving mad watching one of the jazzy Madison Avenue sells of the alphabet and numbers on *Sesame*

Street, or the fast, rock beat of songs about multiplication or grammar. I think it arouses an old anxiety; nothing terrified me more than drills in school—flash cards on which one was supposed to reproduce memorized information.

My natural tendency (and I think this is true of the majority of children) is to absorb things quietly, slowly; through direct experiences; through the processes of gathering associations and ideas. As a child I felt that a great deal was expected of me and I became tense and anxious about measuring up. I was terrified of the processes involved in reading, writing, and arithmetic. It was not really until I was in graduate school that academic learning became truly pleasurable because I was studying what interested me, rather than fulfilling what now seem to me to have been the most ridiculous requirements.

During this past decade, I have discovered that my natural rhythm is to be alone a great deal of the time, to be free to think my own thoughts and learn slowly—using external stimuli (books, lectures, etc.) as an adjunct to exploring my own feelings. I need to be in touch with nature; I cannot be running and doing all the time.

I never knew this as a child. Born into an intellectual environment where great store was set by education and professional life, I set myself goals and a pace of living that were too social, too fast, too demanding. It gave me sinus trouble and frequent colds and backaches as I got older, and mysterious pains in my side that always seemed to be evidence of acute appendicitis but never were—and that disappeared completely, as did other psychosomatic symptoms, with psychotherapy and changing my life style. Now when I run too much, get involved in ambitious and competitive activities, the discomfort hits so hard, so fast, that I am able to extricate myself before the aches and pains can start.

Our daughter was braver than either of her parents; we put up with what we at least felt was expected of us— and, in the process of trying to live up to it, often failed and felt miserable, until we were free to pursue things that interested us so much that our goals became our own. We started out doing the same thing to our child that had been done to us, but she rebelled far more openly and directly— which made us anxious as hell; we'd been so good—how dare she not try to please us as much as we had tried to please our parents!

A bachelor friend of mine had just been to visit his married niece, and was extolling the charms of his grand-nieces and nephews. "Imagine, Eda," he boasted, "Gregory is only two and *he talks like an adult!* And it's all due to *Sesame Street!*" Nothing I can think of is a better example of inappropriate thinking on the part of adults about young children. Parents like to show off; every sign of talent on the part of a child becomes a personal trophy. Approval is a lovely thing to feel as a child, but much too frequently, and especially during the first few years of life, we tend to give approval for tasks that are neither appropriate nor important. If the most important developmental tasks of the preschool period have to do with understanding human frailty and self-acceptance, then the kinds of things that ought to make us proud are any evidence that a child is succeeding in those areas. How I would love to hear a grandparent crowing over the fact that a three-year-old granddaughter was able to talk about feeling angry, or said "I know," when told she was adorable, with the same enthusiasm with which Grandma reports that the entire alphabet has been memorized!

If we are going to give awards, they ought to be for such things as being able to talk about feelings, not being ashamed of being shy or frightened, learning to feel compassion for another child's pain because one has experienced compassion oneself. We should take pride in a child's struggle to discover his own inner pace, his creative abilities, the richness of his imagination. Far more important than the development of academic skills during these early years is the ability to begin to gain control over one's impulses, to behave sensitively toward others, to begin to understand that one is *not* responsible for the unhappy events that occur in the family, and most of all *to be glad to be oneself.*

This is not a negation of the importance or pleasures in ideas, in intellectual achievement. It is simply a question of *what* and *when.* If we have the courage to become introspective about our own early childhood, I think we discover very quickly that if we have feelings of unworthiness, of having failed, they are at least in part due to the fact that we were being judged by the accomplishment of tasks that were appropriate to a different, later, period of growth.

How a human being feels about himself is the axis upon which his whole life will turn. And the most deeply ingrained attitudes—the self-hating parts, the self-loving parts—are pretty well set by five or six years of age. How a human being feels about himself colors everything he feels and does in relation to others as well. It sets the stage for lifetime attitudes about what it means to be a human being. It affects our capacity to use our talents or not, our ability to love, to be responsible citizens.

It is perfectly possible to modify these attitudes later on in life, but if we can avoid crippling distortions in the first place, that seems the wiser choice!

It seems to me that the necessary conclusion one has to come to is that these years are so crucial that they ought to be given a higher priority of adult concern than any later period in growing up. More consistent parental care, more careful training of pediatricians than any other medical specialty, better training and higher salaries for nursery school teachers than for college professors.

Many young men and women who want to be teachers scoff at training in early childhood education; they see it as "baby-sitting," and beneath their dignity. For myself, I cannot imagine *any* higher calling than that of helping a child move toward his school-age years with a deep and abiding sense of his own worth and possibilities.

It seems to me that the highest priority for any government concerned with its own future and the peace of the world community ought to be the facilities it provides for the care and nurturance of young children. If we spent one-tenth as much money on training teachers and providing the best possible preschool child care centers as we spend in a month for war materials and new highway construction, we could change the quality of life for future generations.

It is time for a massive reordering of priorities. For example, one of the most important, required subjects in high school and college ought to be parent education. Free courses in parenting ought to be available to every couple during pregnancy and thereafter through such facilities as day care centers, schools, community groups, and neighborhood centers. The profession I share with a handful of others (most people have no idea what I'm talking about when I say I am a parent educator) ought to become at least as common and well respected as those of bus drivers, plumbers, or policemen. Typical of our current priorities is that at the present time there are no programs for parents on educational television, but plenty on how to cook and take care of plants!

Of course, the personal relationship between parent and child is the crucial issue, and it seems to me that the crux of being most sensitized to the needs of young children is getting into contact with one's own earliest feelings—beginning to parent oneself. That self-nurturance is good for anybody, but it seems to me it is essential for those of us who become parents.

For example now, when I hear a child cry, around lunchtime, on a bus or in a supermarket, I identify immediately with a feeling that is ordinarily repressed very early and usually never recaptured. I begin to have a feeling of such fatigue that I can hardly move; I realize that the sound I am hearing of that child crying is one that only happens in the earliest years, when being tired or hungry can literally make you quite insane. You can't stop, you need desperately to be picked up and carried, you need to be fed and put to bed. Instead your mother or father is saying, "If you don't stop that crying this instant, I'm going to spank you," or "If you don't get up and start walking, I'm just going to leave you right here on the street." You're going crazy, and this person you love and need is telling you to behave rationally! It was only after many years of self-examination that I understood this phenomenon, deep in my gut. When I was a young mother and my daughter behaved in these normal ways, I screamed and threatened. What I now know was happening was that the infantilism she was demonstrating made me anxious as hell; it evoked repressed memories of having once felt exactly the same way—feelings so terrifying, repressed for so long—that the adult goes into a rage at being reminded, begins to behave in equally infantile ways. Before long there are two hysterical babies on the cashier's line!

Now that I recall the feeling, I would behave very differently; if necessary I'd sit right down on the floor of the store or at the street curb, take my child in my arms, and rock her and soothe her. I'd give her something to eat, I'd talk about how it feels when you are little and hungry and tired. We'd rest before we tried to walk on; if necessary, I'd even throw away the damned bag of groceries and carry the child; the feelings are *that* frightening. And even if I felt angry, impatient, embarrassed, tired, at least

I'd *try* and get the words out that would explain what was going on, and that I understood and remembered the feeling. Or if I failed entirely, I'd apologize and explain what was going on later. This is not only "being good" to one's child; it is at long last nurturing the child in oneself. It makes *both* feel better. And that kind of nurturance is the necessary basis for becoming civilized.

NOTE: In this chapter I have tried to write about early child development from the vantage point of my own inner experience. That is, of course, only part of the picture. I have written at length—and I think quite well!—on this subject elsewhere, especially in *How to Survive Parenthood* (New York: Random House, 1965) and *The Conspiracy Against Childhood* (New York: Atheneum, 1967).

Chapter 3

We all come into the grade-school years with some residue of our earliest misperceptions as well as both conscious and unconscious messages from our parents and other adults about our real or imagined shortcomings. And there we are, with all our vulnerability hanging out, faced with the second major task of growing up: How do you take this self you have become and begin to learn about living among all the others who share your life experiences?

One of my clearest memories of childhood is when Emily came into our fourth-grade class. She was the only new child that year, all the rest of us having known each other for two or three years. She was a giant—even taller than

Lester, the tallest boy in the class, who was having his own troubles. His voice had changed when he was eight and he was a baritone, so that when we had music class, he could be an endless source of amusement and derision.

My recollection is that I was the fattest girl in the class, and that I viewed myself as a monstrosity. I felt that this handicap excluded me from ever being accepted by the high society of the class—a very rich girl whose father made movies, a handsome boy who was her cousin, the most beautiful and smartest girl in the class, and two boys who were nine-year-old jocks. When I look at photographs of myself at eight or nine, all I see is a kind of a cute little girl, on the chubby side—maybe five pounds overweight. But I felt like a hippopotamus, and nothing happened to make me change that perception of myself.

Under those circumstances, I was *delighted* when Emily wet her pants. It was an ordinary day—I wasn't understanding multiplication any better than I had the day before, and I was, as usual, dying of jealousy because Phyllis and Stewart were in love. Suddenly, there was a kind of electricity in the air. The teacher, who always had a bright red nose—I never found out why—called on Emily to answer some question. It was about the second or third week Emily had been in our class, and she hadn't said a word. She was the shyest girl I'd ever seen. I suppose the teacher felt it was time to try to help her participate in the group. At any rate, we quickly realized that all our worse nightmares for ourselves had come true in Emily's case. There was a great sense of relief. It had happened—but not to any of the rest of us.

Emily lived with that nightmare fulfilled for the rest of the school years; she did not return the following fall. I worry and wonder about her often. I try to reassure myself that sooner or later being labeled as "the girl who wet her pants in fourth grade" wore off, or if it didn't, that she got professional help with her memories of that awful year.

What I learned from probing my own past was that the distinguishing feature about the grade school years, from about six to twelve, is their terrible cruelty. In spite of the fact that I attended one of the best of the pioneering experimental, progressive private schools of that era (the 1920s and 1930s) I have many painful memories. I had some loving, insightful teachers; I was offered a smorgasbord of activities—music, art, shop, creative writing, nature study. Classes rarely if ever had more than twenty students in them.

The things I remember with nostalgia and pleasure were being in plays, a creative writing club, and ethics classes, where we discussed moral and ethical issues in daily living. As I look back, I think that last was the best part of the program, because it filled our deepest needs. These are the years for finding out about other people, about living with others—of relating that self one discovered in the first five years to being a member of a group of one's peers. Children are *starving* for guidance, for principles, to help them deal with this challenge.

Many of my memories are unhappy ones, and if that was

the case in one of the best schools ever designed, it seems easy to understand what awful things must happen to children in the general run of schools—especially today, with so much more to be learned, so much emphasis on facts, the enormous advances in science and technology with which we were not burdened then. How much worse it must also be, now, when even young children often feel there is nothing good to hope for.

When I finally learned to read—and what a trauma that was—I was given books that idealized life and made me believe that I was a very lucky little girl, indeed, because in my lifetime all the terrible tragedies of the past would be undone. There was a series of books, Twins in Other Lands, that told about life in foreign countries. Before I had been born there had been a terrible world war, but it had been fought to end all wars, forever, and now I would grow up in perfect harmony with children everywhere.

The curriculum in fourth grade had to do with ancient Greece and the beginning of democracy. A few years ago my husband informed me that the Classical Greek period lasted only about fifty years; the shock almost gave me a heart attack. I had been under the impression it had lasted for several hundred years. When he also told me that there were slaves in Socrates' time, I simply didn't believe him; I could recall nothing like that in the books I was given to read. Democracy had been discovered, and was the perfect form of government; a recent war had now made it possible for us to have peace forever. There were, I vaguely recall, some problems with unemployment and union members being shot by the police, and men selling apples on a corner near my school, but President Roosevelt was going to take care of these minor matters. All was well with the world. I don't recall feeling that the lot of Negroes and Indians left much to be desired. Lincoln had freed the slaves and Indians wove blankets and danced on reservations.

Despite having a relatively happy environment, we were cruel and mean to each other. Small cliques formed for the sole purpose of ganging up on a few other kids, to make their lives miserable. I have a memory of walking by the playground almost daily in misery, because some bigger girls in the next grade teased me. One of my most painful memories took place on the Mall in Central Park. I was trying to learn to skate, and was about as well coordinated as a rag doll; I fell down a lot. A group of children were laughing at me one day, and as I fell for the seventh or eighth time, they formed a laughing, teasing circle around me. Nobody was hurting me, and as I look back now I know it was a very mild form of meanness, but at the time I became hysterical with terror and began sobbing. The other children looked puzzled, then frightened, and ran away. Any time I have felt demeaned or anxious about my own worth, that memory recurs.

In the sixth grade, when Amy was going through puberty and I now had a sort of gang of my own, we sent her anonymous letters about how she stank; as others began to menstruate, we would peer over the tops of the toilet cubicles and shriek with laughter. We had a teacher who had terrible dandruff, and we spent hours making fun of him behind his back. There was a boy in my class who blushed very easily, and we teased him mercilessly to watch him turn crimson.

Most of the time it was a jungle, full of rivalry, jealousy, feelings of unworthiness and inadequacy, each of us sure that everyone else was happier than we were.

I remember one episode in which we stopped hurting each other and stood together. I think it was in second grade. There was a lovely child in our class who was never mean and who seemed to love all of us. I suspect that because he had been born with a serious heart condition, he had received a great deal of love and had never been expected to compete with anyone, so he had turned into a civilized human being, even at seven. He had bright rosy cheeks, but he seemed quite frail and he missed school a great deal of the time. One day our teacher told us he was too sick ever to come back to school, but that he missed us very much. She proposed to take us on a walk. We would stop on the street where he lived, and he would see us from his apartment house window. We stood across the street, so he could see us clearly, and we all waved. I think we knew he was going to die. For many of us it must have been our first experience with death, much less the death of someone our own age—and I recall that day and the days that followed as happier days, strange as that may sound. We were sad and frightened about Bobby, but somehow this event drew us together in a new way; for a brief time we were kind to one another. With a common tragedy we were able to transcend our separate insecurities, and I can still recall that warm sense of communal sharing.

It couldn't possibly last because even in that superior school our cruelty was encouraged. Competition was deeply rooted in the climate of our group life. Although the business of not giving grades or marks was beginning, little was done to really convince us that we were not competing with each other.

One memory tells this story vividly. I have a cousin with whom I had an unusually close relationship; we were more like sisters. We started in first grade together, and really loved each other. She gave me more security and confidence than I might otherwise have had. In the beginning of second grade she was so far ahead in reading and writing that she was skipped into a third-grade class. I was devastated—not only to lose a source of comfort, but because from that moment on our relationship was always corrupted and scarred by her being "the smart one" and me "the dumb one."

Although we played together almost daily after school, it was never quite the same. During adolescence, when we were both faced with the monumental life-and-death problem of how to be popular with boys, we clung to each other, but I still felt separated by her being one month younger and one grade ahead. Maybe that was one of the factors that made me more competitive, more ambitious, in later years.

In any event, one day we were both in the girls' bathroom. Each cubicle had double swinging doors, and my cousin got banged on the head coming out. She really hurt herself, and I recalled feeling terribly guilty about it. I never forgot it. She doesn't remember that event at all. What I feel when I think about it is both compassion and pleasure. I really felt bad when I saw her tears and the bump on her head. But in some part of me, I was also glad she was getting hers! The competition set in motion by the school's setting a higher value on her academic achievement, created for many years an insurmountable rift of deep rivalry.

We are still friends and, in our fifties, have talked about those times. My cousin tells me that she envied me—that she remembers me as having more friends, being less shy. I am sure the separation and the labeling caused her suffering, too.

It didn't have to happen. It seems to me that the best of more recent educational experimentations is being done in gradeless classrooms, where children with perhaps a three- or four-year age range share some common and some separate learning experiences. In such a setting, one can reinforce the idea that each individual has his own gifts and rate of growing; that no one is in competition with anyone else; that the only useful kind of striving is for the best in oneself.

What actually happens is that children who already have all kinds of emotionally crippling feelings of inadequacy and unworthiness find themselves trying to work on the problems of group life in an atmosphere filled with danger —each child pitted against all others in a never-ending race for approval and success that is unreal and irrelevant. Everybody simply *can't* be ahead of everyone else, but that is what we are constantly asking our children to believe.

Of course I would like to believe that a time will come when adults will be so perceptive and sensitive to the needs of infants, toddlers, and preschoolers that children will come into grade school with far less hidden agenda of self-hatred expressing itself in ganging up on even more vulnerable victims. Until that lucky day—and I'm not exactly holding my breath—we need to devise school settings in which it is simply not possible for cruelty to be tolerated, much less encouraged, as it is today.

At the present time almost everything about our elementary schools does encourage children to be confirmed in their poor judgments of themselves and thereby reinforced in their meanness to others. Whom do we value the most? The kid with the highest marks; the one who can memorize best; the one who complies most obsequiously with the teacher's demands; the one with good penmanship; the one who gets the most answers right to the flash cards; the one who throws a baseball faster and harder; the one who has the most "perfect features"?

I was watching a segment of the television program "To Tell the Truth," because as I turned it on I saw that someone I'd heard of, an educator, was one of the three people to be identified. He was being questioned about a new experimental school he had founded, of which I'd heard and greatly admired. The school is a genuine community, in which everyone is encouraged to feel needed by everyone else. Various kinds of farming and mechanical training are given to all, in order to feed and run the school. Students are offered a broad range of studies, but eventually choose the one or two subjects that seem to give them most self-direction and sense of personal fulfillment. After much of this had been ascertained by the panel, one of them said, "Number Two, I get the impression that your school must get mostly maladjusted children."

I thought to myself, That sums up the prevailing attitude toward education, succinctly and clearly; if it's a community of mutual concern, without grades and marks, aimed at self-growth, it's gotta be for sick kids!

If we would only understand what our goals have *got to be,* we would insist that every grade school and high school child in the country had an opportunity for that kind of learning.

There is a series of books by Judy Blume about children of grade school age that seems to me to be a marvelously accurate picture of the complex human relations that develop out of individual insecurity. In one of her books, *Blubber,** a class is being unspeakably cruel to one of its members during music class. The teacher threatens to punish the class by failing them in the course. One girl wonders if cruelty can go on your permanent record, bringing a fate worse than death because "it could keep you out of college." That is some statement of values; it isn't how you treat each other that matters, or your lives right here, in this moment of time—it's that old devil "getting ahead" that

* New York: Bradbury Press, 1947.

matters, somewhere off in a vague future. It did not surprise me at all that so many of the Watergate felons were "brilliant students"—as I recall, there were even a couple of Phi Beta Kappas in that motley crew; where else but in school do we really make it clear that power and winning are far more important than how you get there? What we ought to be teaching children is that it doesn't matter if you know how to read and write if you can't discriminate between good ideas and lousy ones, between honest people and liars and cheats; between dangerous demagogues and statesmen. We need to teach children that power is dangerous unless used responsibly for the good of all and that personal success is not measured in relation to how many people you've beaten, but to what degree you are able to use your own gifts, creatively.

The fact of the matter is that all the grading and testing of children is of no use whatsoever in predicting later potentials or performance. I never actually failed—because I was in a progressive school! My husband, on the other hand, failed frequently. Both of us have clear recollections of the people in our classes whom we envied—the smart ones who got good grades. They may all be leading happy and exemplary lives, but not very many have led as interesting lives as we have, or struggled harder to use every last drop of their capacities.

A few years ago, when I appeared on a television program in a midwestern city, a woman called the station and asked to speak to me. She turned out to be a girl who had been in my class for twelve years. I had really hated her;

she *never* failed any test, had an A or a B average in every single subject, and never struggled the way I did over homework or got nervous about taking tests. I hadn't seen her since graduation from high school, and we arranged to meet at the airport for lunch before I came home. The meeting was a revelation! She was one of the dullest people I'd ever met. Most of the lunchtime was spent in her complaining about how terribly her children were turning out because they didn't want to go to college. She had gone to college. She'd married immediately thereafter, and had been a housewife ever since. She didn't seem to have any special interests or enthusiasms. It was a dreadful reunion, but it confirmed what I already knew—that school achievement bears no relationship whatsoever to adult performance. In fact, the most creative children often have the worst school records. Under such circumstances, comparisons between children not only harm them individually and in their relations with one another, they are also utterly useless. The only measurement that serves any purpose is the child's own growth and change. If tests are used for evaluation, they ought to be used to help the individual child assess his own development, the areas in which he needs help, his weaknesses and strengths. What matters is what the child can learn about himself. If various methods of self-rating could be instituted, the resulting reduction in anxiety and tension would make it possible for students to tolerate any necessary objective judgments that must eventually be made for the measurement of aptitude and information in special areas of professional training. In order to find out if a twenty-year-old has the qualifications for entrance into medical school, it is neither necessary nor useful to start testing him at the age of five! Until sixteen or seventeen none of the results will mean anything, since interest, motivation, degree of anxiety about test taking, capacity to accept the rules of the test game, all tend to be quite erratic until the young person is in the process of clarifying his ultimate goals.

What I learned about education and testing from my own growing up is that a relatively small percentage of the children who were high achievers still were when they were adults. And that many of us who thought we were stupid turned out to be pretty damned smart!

My husband went to a perfectly terrible public school, where competing for grades was all you went to school for. At one time, during exam week, he made a mistake about the attendance rules. He had understood the principal to say that on any day you didn't have a test, you could stay home. He stayed home one day, and the principal, in order to make it clear that a serious crime had been committed, told the class who had done it and then punished everyone by making them stay after school hours. For the rest of the school year, Larry had to walk home three miles out of his way in order to avoid being beaten up by some of the other children in his class. The principal was a sadist, who was fired several years later for some other act of violence in which some more secure child was able to fight back, I guess. But whenever I think about that awful hike, I am reminded of how quickly children take their cues from adults.

Rivalries and jealousies are inevitable in any human relationships, but what schools and parents frequently do is fan the flames of group tension by setting competitive goals and encouraging children to think of one another as the enemy.

An interesting experiment in a number of schools in recent years has been to choose some of the poor readers in sixth grade to help teach the children who are having difficulty learning to read in second grade. What happens is that both children improve. Given a chance to relate cooperatively and compassionately, children blossom. The poor readers know instinctively what would be hard for the second graders to understand; they've been there themselves. Both children are allowed to experience their difficulties together, without shame. With less tension and more mutual affection, their shared problems begin to be solved.

If one accepts the premise that the primary developmental task of grade school-age children is socialization, the advent of the clique and the gang begin to take on a different significance. They are attempts—often not very successful and quite rough—at cooperation. Within one's own group it is possible to become compassionate and cooperative; competition is against outside groups, not against each other. If our educational system allowed for it, classes could be clubs! A special friendship arrangement—a place for a person to take his troubles, openly, without fear.

Several years ago I wrote a book entitled *What Makes*

Me Feel This Way? * It is written for children about seven to twelve years of age. I have gotten a great deal of mail from teachers, telling me of their experiences in reading it with a class and using it as a basis for discussion. The book deals with feelings, all kinds—the kinds I had myself when I was that age, the kind all children have—sometimes without even knowing it, sometimes secretively—fears, confusions, angers, jealousies. In every case, what astounded the children was that every other child in the class had the same feelings he or she had. What a rotten system of education we have, when children who are trying so hard to find decent, reasonable ways of relating to each other are not taught about their *common feelings*! Nothing unites human beings in greater understanding than finding out they all have similar kinds of feelings; nothing sets a better foundation for human compassion and cooperation.

We do everything possible to interfere with this kind of communication instead of fostering it. A little girl is secretly whispering to her neighbor about being worried because her mother is sick; the teacher reprimands them for talking while she's teaching the multiplication table. A sweet little boy is clandestinely trying to explain a spelling rule to another child who is all confused on a spelling test—and the teacher gives them both zeros for "cheating."

There we are, in that elementary classroom, the drama of civilization at hand: How do a group of individuals learn to live together? And instead of giving them the tools of insight, understanding, communal responsibility,

* New York: Macmillan, 1972.

and concern, we turn them against one another with labels, with scores—accentuating every feeling of anxiety and insecurity, feeding the tendency to be cruel.

Most important of all, we do very little about teaching children practical techniques of democratic living. It seems to me classes ought to be discussing some issue and voting on it several times a week! There ought to be more opportunities for committee work, for the delegation of responsibility, for battling out different opinions and needs. Every classroom ought to be a town meeting!

My happiest memories of the grade school years are about *doing* things with other kids. The horrible memories are sitting at a desk trying to understand, memorize, take tests. Luckily I had both. I cannot *imagine* how children less fortunate than I manage to live through the school years, without more of the doing.

I will always have a deep, empathic relationship with the Cave Dwellers, as we called Neanderthal Man in second grade. The reason for this is that one day our teacher took us to Central Park, where we collected some large stones, which we took back to the cooking classroom (an innovative feature of progressive education in the 1920s). There we put the stones in the oven, got them good and hot, then took them out with a shovel and placed them on sheets of asbestos under the tables, which we covered with brown cloths. Then we put slabs of beef on the stones, and by God they *cooked*! We had actually cooked food in exactly the way people had done it millions of years ago, in their caves. It wasn't only a strong identification with humans of another time. Because it was so totally absorbing, I forgot my self-consciousness with other children. In having a wonderful time, without any element of competition, we were learning to enjoy being part of a group, and giving pleasure to each other merely because we were experiencing something directly, together.

A second identification with a historical period occurred when we were studying medieval times. We had a project of building a three-paneled screen for our classroom. It was a big room, and the teacher wanted a divider so a small group could have an opportunity to work quietly, away from the rest of the class. The two or three best artists in the class made a rough sketch on the wood of various Gothic scenes, and all of us painted some part of the screen. The finished product seemed unbelievably beautiful. I can still remember the costumes, the vivid colors, the gilt edges, the castles and horses. All of it belonged to all of us. We did it together.

When we had to play competitive games in the park, I immediately regressed into feelings of unworthiness. On those occasions when we were allowed "free play," I had a wonderful time. There were some wonderful rock formations in the park, and we acted out "Tarzan" stories. We were lost in a world of imagination in which we were free of all comparisons with each other, as we perceived our "real" selves. I remember these as times when I felt completely accepted, successful. We didn't fight, we didn't hurt each other's feelings, when we played our own games.

The worst side of all of us appeared when we were most

in competition with each other, whether in sports or in the classroom. When I could not answer quickly enough during a math drill, I began to make fun of the boy sitting next to me, who had wax in his ears and a runny nose; when the teacher reprimanded him, he "accidentally" spilled ink on my story, which the teacher had read to the class and had said was the best story about a knight she had ever read. Such memories convince me that when children are most cruel to each other, adults have pitted them against each other.

Play is just as important during this second stage of growing up as it was in the first period. The preschooler must play in order to figure out what it means to be an individual human person; the school-age child needs to play in order to begin to figure out how to relate to other people. Schools are crazy places from this point of view. You sit at a desk listening to a teacher for three or four hours and then you have a fifteen-minute recess. Because there is usually so little interaction allowed in the classroom, that fifteen-minute recess has to serve as the only laboratory for experimenting with give-and-take. By the time recess comes around, the children are so full of anger at having to compete so hard, and so restless from sitting still, that recess is full of battles.

Play ought to be a central focus for all learning. Every other animal learns by playing. Unfortunately, the human animal is the only one that tries hard to interfere with child's play. Allowed to follow natural drives and instincts, children tend to *work* very hard in their play. They want to find things out; they want to develop all kinds of mental and physical skills. What they need around them are adults who are adventurers, who can respond to their vitality, their curiosity, and *help them to find out what they want to learn and learn it.* You need to read and write to learn about interesting things and to express your ideas; you need to add and subtract to go shopping, to measure, to figure out how to play some games. You need all kinds of information and skills to build a model airplane or go on a camping trip or understand space travel. School-age children *want* these skills, but they learn them best in a climate of active disorder. Peace and quiet and a carefully organized environment may be comfortable and constructive for adults, but not for most children. They need to move around, to *do*, themselves—not listen to secondhand reports.

What happens is that children assume adults are right, simply because they are grownups. If parents and teachers tell you it is necessary and right to sit quietly and listen, you assume they know what they are talking about. Imagine what might happen if a teacher were to tell a child, "You can't study arithmetic today because you didn't do well at recess"! A totally different message, speaking to the child's need to learn to relate to others, as central and essential—all else being peripheral to that. The mind boggles at imagining how much higher a level of good citizenship might grow out of that orientation!

"Guided chaos" is the way work and play need to be interwoven in a child's life. It takes highly skilled, patient, dedicated teaching. So what? That's possible. It seems worth trying if the end result might be a generation who had some better ways of relating to each other than bitter competition and outbursts of violence.

In one imaginative educational experiment, an elementary school class was told they had to meet certain inflexible criteria for graduation into the next grade. The teachers had decided all the necessary information and skills could be learned (memorized) in six to eight weeks. They were going to spend all the rest of the year doing things that really interested the children. They had all sorts of classroom projects, individual research, lots of trips, building and cooking, and so on. For the last month and a half of the school year they did nothing but drill for the required tests. More children passed easily than in any of the other classes in the same grade in the same school who had followed the traditional curriculum all year.

I learned as many stupid and useless facts as most children—the capital of North Dakota, the main industries of Norway, the year of Custer's Last Stand, how many tablespoons in a pint. I forgot them all. Any time I need to know them, I can look them up in about forty seconds.

What children need to learn are the fundamental skills involved in reasoning, knowing where to go to find something out, making connections between ideas. Nature meant them to find these things out actively; that is what play is all about. Of course, play for some children *is* to read, to explore numbers, to study quietly, exploring ideas: we simply need a wider range of alternatives.

There was one place in my childhood that was different

from anything else. It seems to me that in this oasis I never felt dumb or ugly, and I never needed a scapegoat or a clique to make me feel more secure. It was truly a society in which individual talents were explored and appreciated without competition with others, and it was therefore possible for a group of children to genuinely care about each other. There were exceptions, of course—children with special problems who were not happy—but on the whole it was a place of joy for many of us.

The place was Westport, Connecticut, a summer colony of cottages. The group of families that first came there included a number of remarkable educators, pioneers in experimental education. Their names are a hall of fame in the history of education. They were colleagues of my mother's, and all had school-age children. They formed and ran a summer day camp, and hired a spectacular staff of teachers to serve as counselors. It was an intimate, family-oriented, safe, consistent, ongoing experience through many of my years of growing up until I became a counselor myself. It was a program designed for pleasure, so there were no anxieties about having to learn; as a result, I know I learned far more important things there—about myself, about the kinds of people I admired, about living with other people my age.

I remember a particularly rainy summer when one of our main projects was making puppets. I was very good at sculpting heads, making masks. Our counselor was a woman by the name of Adele Franklin, who became the director of a project in New York City known as the All-

Day Neighborhood Schools, one of the most important and child-loving programs ever undertaken by the Board of Education. I didn't know she was one of the great educators of the time, then; all I knew was that she thought each of us was wonderful; that, in her presence, I glowed, expanded, became more myself. I remember that as we worked on the puppets we all talked—about everything and anything —and wherever our explorations led us, Adele followed. The next summer we ran a community store, and I, who spent my entire childhood failing and hating arithmetic, had no difficulty at all working on the store's accounts, making change, understanding wholesale and retail prices. I *loved* organizing the merchandise and selling, and so the incidental learnings of a mathematical nature didn't scare me at all. That same year we worked most of the summer on a play in which I had a lead part, and in which all of us worked on building sets, making costumes—I think we even wrote our own script.

The most competitive game we played was "Kick the Can." It is the only group game I can remember from childhood without a feeling of dread and mortification. I was having so much fun, I felt so safe with the other children, that I just never felt clumsy and fat, as I did during the winter. I loved hiding in the high bushes near the camp house, and running out to kick the can on the rock before being tagged. I was too busy to wonder if I would do it well.

Behind our house was a running brook with large stepping stones. A tree had fallen across the brook and we had a hammock there. We also had a raft. I spent long hours lying on the raft or on a big flat rock, writing poetry. It wasn't for anybody but me. My hours were quiet and secret for the most part, and when, as an adult, I struggled to come back to the enjoyment of solitude, I know that these years of childhood were what I knew I could return to, and gave me the courage and hope to relearn how to play, alone. Looking back, it seems to me that this was one of the few places where I never felt hurried or judged. I remember it with joy and a sense of having gotten enormous sustenance from it. Without any pressures to meet other people's expectations, I really had a chance to explore who *I* was. It became the source of most of my adult play-work pleasures— ceramics, writing, dramatics, working with young children, parent education.

I slept on a porch on a lower level near the brook. There were no windows—just screens. I could hear the brook; when it rained, it was almost like being right in it. I remember sunsets, when my brother and I would be walking along the road, waiting for the sight of our car bringing my mother and father home from the city. We would shriek with delight, and we were allowed to hang on, standing on the running board, while my father drove slowly to our house.

One of the children had a tent, where we slept often. There were all kinds of adventures, cookouts, evening swims. At one point we formed ourselves into a dramatic game of "Robin Hood and his Merry Men," and enacted all kinds of stories, including Robin Hood and Maid Marion getting married. (We were a conservative crew!) I made the wedding veil of entwined daisies. I don't recall our ganging up on one particular child, or of my feeling envious of any others because they were better than I thought I was. Each of us was being encouraged to do our own thing.

There was one exception to this idyllic life. One summer we had a counselor who was very gung ho on swimming. Until that time, I adored being in the water, but now we had to pass tests, have our names on charts, compete in races, etc. We were also required to learn to dive, and I was simply not well enough coordinated to feel comfortable about it; I obviously was not ready to try it. It became a contest of wills between myself and the counselor. Finally, one afternoon she told me I couldn't go home until I dived off the board. I was terrified. She waited me out. After several hours I finally fell off the board in some semblance of a knee dive, which satisfied her. For the rest of the summer I hated swimming and to this day, absolutely *nothing* could get me to dive off a board. It was the only arbitrary demand made on me in three summers of joy, and the only "learning" that never took.

And there was so much learning going on! I went to the Westport library every week; it was the beginning of an insatiable hunger for reading. Suddenly reading was for fun, not to pass any tests. It was my first awareness that books could make you cry—the years of Elsie Dinsmore refusing to play the piano on the Sabbath, and Beth dying in *Little Women*. I feel a sense of wonder and shock, just recalling this—that with no one checking up on my reading, I was free to experience the magic of identification with imaginary people.

I think the essence of these special years—when I was truly allowed to experience *myself*—was a time when I was driving home with my parents and there was a thunderstorm. The sun came out as the storm ended, and there was a rainbow. I asked to get out of the car, and asked my father for some paper and a pencil—right then and there I needed to write a poem about the rainbow! My parents sat patiently in the car, waiting for me to conclude my "Peak Experience." * That's the way the summers were; some deep fertilization going on, of the best there was in me. The older I grow, the more it seems to me that those summers were more important than almost any other group learning experience. When each child/person is allowed to explore himself most fully, relationships with others seem to fall into place. You become free to enjoy living and working with others. Love begins. I remember those other children with special tenderness, and with almost none of the tension and anxiety that was part of so many other group experiences.

The preoccupation with sex began when I was about eleven. Until that time our interest was spasmodic—occasional episodes of the giggles over nudity and hysterical concern with hiding ourselves. But not an awful lot; since our parents were liberated and relaxed, we were well-in-

* A phrase used by the psychologist, Dr. Abraham Maslow, to describe a special moment of creativity and self-actualization.

formed about where babies came from, and free to be undressed in front of each other if we felt like it. That particular year there was one very well-informed boy in our group. He was a nephew of a family that lived in the colony, so he was an outsider who had not been with us the previous summers. I suppose he needed a wedge into our closed circle—and he sure had it! He knew hundreds of dirty jokes, and every evening, after supper, we sophisticates in the oldest group would gather 'round for our daily initiation into what we conceived to be adulthood! In fifty-three years of living I have never heard racier tales than his. He was in the avant-garde, forty years ahead of his time on pornography. But every single thing I learned from him was in some way a distortion, a misconception! The following fall I repeated all his stories to my friends in seventh grade. The harder we laughed, the less we understood the story.

Looking back, I have the feeling that this was a necessary stage in growing up. It was a sort of ritualistic ceremony, playing a part, going through motions that would lead to a next step. I think adults tend to read too much into such childish experimentation. It sounds awfully sophisticated and knowledgeable. It was also the time for a preoccupation with kissing games, and in both instances it was our naïveté and ignorance that made it possible for us to put on such a good act. The more we learned, the more we really matured, the less we needed such games—the more embarrassing they became. Innocence often appears to be depravity!

I often think of those sessions when I hear about some

new and colorful version of swinging couples. I think their level of sexual development is on a par with what we were experiencing! Sex becomes less preoccupied with technical details when we become mature enough to handle the complexities of loving.

Listening to dirty jokes was a form of play, but one that was not as significant a part of my development as the other kinds of play during these summers. Mostly it was discovering my own talents and interests and the beginnings of a special relationship with the natural world around me.

Whenever I leave the monastic life I usually lead when I am writing, it takes me days to get back to work. One weekend off, one dinner party, and the rhythm is gone. My husband came up to our home on the Cape last weekend, and when he left I was back to feeling lonesome and disconnected from my work. Once upon a time I would have started to read technical, professional books because I thought that would discipline my mind and get me back in shape to work.

What I did yesterday was this: First I went to our friendly neighborhood nursery and bought a yellow rosebush and some portulaca for a rock garden. I also bought some new birdseed. Then I ordered a cooked lobster, all for myself, and spent about half an hour cracking it, getting thoroughly slopped up in the process of extricating the meat. During that meal I put on some records—favorite old musicals seemed to be what I was in the mood for—*On a Clear Day, Once Upon a Mattress, Bells Are Ringing.* During my planting, I took a good look at a rhododendron bush in full flower, and gasped inwardly at the perfection of each blossom. I cut one, with all the leaves around it, shaped like a star and put it in a flat dish on my desk, and just sat and looked at it for awhile. Anyone who has done this knows what an intricate miracle such a flower is. Having filled the bird feeders, I discovered much to my surprise that my bobwhites were right outside my window, although it was now midafternoon and the music was blaring. Usually they are shy and appear only for a few minutes at dawn. They are devotedly attentive and romantic with each other, and it's refreshing to see a couple in love and know they won't get a divorce, no matter what! I had also bought myself some sculpting clay, and as I sat, looking out the window, fooling around with it, I noticed a tiny goldfinch drinking at the birdbath. At one point he lost his balance and fell in. I laughed out loud when, instead of flying away, he decided to make the best of it and had himself a splashing bath while he was there.

By the end of the day I felt wonderfully refreshed, had a good night's sleep, and got back to work the next day. What I was doing was *playing*. A grownup version of what a child does naturally. *I was pleasuring myself.* It is not self-centered, and it is not anti-intellectual. Such play is the beginning of concern for others and the necessary step toward thinking creatively—making use of ideas, exploring new facts, integrating learning in such a way that it is not something that merely bombards you from the outside, but becomes part of your being. We learn best the skills for such refreshment when we feel at home with ourselves and safe with others.

Even more than school, family life offers opportunities to learn about living with others. Lasting lessons about cooperation and shared living are going on at home during these years of growing. We all need to be more alert about what it is we may be teaching.

One of the best lessons I ever learned about being an individual in a group occurred when I was about eleven years old. I got rheumatic fever and had to go to bed for a number of months. It could have been a devastating experience, but it wasn't. I think of it as the time the family rallied to meet my needs, and we all ended up having something special in our lives.

One of the projects initiated by my parents was that we should have a family newspaper, of which I would be editor. In the course of each week my parents and brother would submit articles, stories, poems, letters to the editor, and editorials to me, in my bed. I would paste all the pieces together, make headlines and illustrations, and one night a week we had a family gathering in my room to read *The Bed Post* together. We were all natural writers—and funny, too—and the few issues that still remain are full of affection and enjoyment of one another.

My parents got me going on a wide assortment of projects. I became fascinated with planting various kinds of seeds—grapefruit and orange seeds, I remember, especially. I had a window sill full of plants. I had a small loom and I wove scarves. I knitted, I wrote story books; my brother and

I gave original plays in my bedroom. When the siege finally ended and I was fully recovered, I had a big sale of everything I'd grown and made and written. All the family and friends were invited, and the proceeds were given to the Playschools Association, where my mother worked, an organization devoted to providing poor city children with good play programs in the summertime and after school.

What I found out was that it always feels good to be doing useful things for other people, and that I was important to people who loved me.

These are also the years when children learn about life with others through sibling relationships. The first thing I remember about my brother was the day he was born. I was sitting on a potty in the living room, early in the morning, when my father raced into the house and up the stairs, shouting to our maid, "It's a boy! It's a boy!" Having never as yet read any books by Freud (I was only four at the time, after all), I did not know I was supposed to feel "penis envy." In all my thousands of hours of psychotherapy, I was never able, no matter how hard I tried, to make anything more significant out of that introduction other than that my father was happy to now have a daughter *and* a son. Since girls in my family were encouraged to become all they could be, I never felt any disadvantage in being female; my mother was a living example of the pleasures in unlimited possibilities.

As things turned out, my brother has a sense of humor which is a source of delight to me. At my parent's fiftieth wedding anniversary party my brother introduced me by saying, "My sister and I had a normal sibling relationship; she tried to kill me!" This is absolutely not true; I only *thought* I'd tried to kill him. When he was about three, we were playing in Central Park, next to the lake. My brother had a boat, but the string broke and the boat sailed away. I must have yelled, "Catch it!" because he leaned too far out and fell in. The water was three or four feet deep. A man on the shore jumped into the water with all his clothes on and fished him out. As an adult, recalling the experience, I realized that I hadn't pushed him but that I had probably wanted to! Everytime I pass the little cupola-like building on West Seventy-Seventh Street from which we were sailing our boats, I am reminded of the human frailty of ambivalent feelings. All things considered, I think we managed to grow up within the normal range of love-hate sibling relations.

I must admit I didn't make life easy for him. In the fifth grade I was studying the Middle Ages, and when I found out about knights and squires, I explained it all to my brother, and somehow sweet-talked him into the idea that I should dub him my knight, which I did with a wooden sword, as he kneeled. I explained that he had to do whatever I told him, and the poor kid fell for it—at least for a while. I also cheated so terribly at Monopoly that I put him in a dreadful bind. One day he had to go to the bathroom desperately, but he was so afraid I'd cheat that he raced back, fell on a highly waxed floor—and broke his arm. I myself have always been a "safety-prone" individual. One day we were walking down a hill and there was a great stretch of smooth ice in front of us. I said I thought it would be wonderful fun to slide on it, but I didn't do it—he did. I think that time he needed a couple of stitches in his chin.

There were years in which we barely tolerated each other's existence. I remember his revolting knickers and socks always falling down, and his runny nose. I also remember that he was a real miser, kept his allowance under his mattress—but that he could sometimes be wheedled into lending me money.

I loved writing plays, and he and I gave performances when our parents had company. We'd hang a sheet across the living room for a curtain. We made costumes and scenery. I was in charge, but I always knew I needed him or there wouldn't be any fun.

Four times especially I knew how much I loved him. The first was when we were both sent to a sleepaway camp when he was only three. It was too soon, and we were both homesick; I was flooded with pity for him. The second time was a few years later. I came home from school and found him lying on his bed, quiet and scared. Nobody was home. He'd been bitten by a dog. I called the doctor and took him to the doctor's office. He had to have awful, painful rabies shots in his abdomen every day, since we could not find the dog. I felt enormously protective and strong when I got home, but later felt deeply shaken by the responsibility. It was an experience in mothering.

The third time was when I "helped" him to avoid eating

the hot cereal he despised each morning. (I had escaped this fate by being overweight.) I suggested he throw the cereal out the window. There was a rooftop terrace below us, and that's where the cereal fell. He would probably never have been caught, since the rain and snow washed the cereal away—but he always put raisins in his cereal, and they began to pile up! When the neighbors complained, I was in a panic that he would say it had been my idea, but he didn't. I was overwhelmed with gratitude and love. Between the influence of my brother and my father, I seem always to have been attracted to sweet, gentle men. How lucky I've been; how often my husband has taken the blame for my raisins!

The fourth time was when my brother got infantile paralysis. Sheer terror! I could not imagine my life without him, and the thought that he might be permanently crippled was unendurable. The relief of his homecoming, recovered, was so great that I don't believe we had a fight— for weeks.

Because I was four years older, our relationship gave me more confidence and freedom than it did him. I did not feel competitive because I could do things first, so the competition was harder on him. Where I often felt inadequate away from home, being the oldest at home, with an often sweet and compliant brother, gave me confidence, a sense of power. The loving and hating feelings, the rivalry, and the way each of us reacted, surely colored our later relations with men and women, especially with our respective spouses. But the essence of it was that both of us were learning about being individuals in a group. There were regular family meetings to decide important issues, long debates, and serious voting. One issue I remember was our complaint that when we went on vacation my father did not stop the car at the very next gas station when we said we had to go to the bathroom. We won the argument; from that time on he had to stop. I think we must have given such a heartrending performance that our mother decided to cast her vote with our side!

We were different; we were each loved. We had both separate and joint relationships with our parents, grandparents, uncles, and aunts. Sometimes having each other was fun; other times it was a nuisance. Sometimes we loved, sometimes we tolerated, sometimes we hated—but the good times outweighed the bad, and the lessons in cooperation and sharing have enhanced our relationships with other people. We learned a lot about give and take; we learned it was good to love and be loved.

Whatever the family constellation—an only child with two parents, or five kids with one parent—lessons are constantly being learned about community life. Children *want* responsibility; they want to be needed. The less they are compared and the less they are expected to love each other, the more likely they are to care for each other. It never occurred to me that I should be like my brother. I do not recall ever feeling I was supposed to love him all the time. Those two factors enhanced the possibility for us to grow up caring about each other.

It was during the grade school years, especially, that I

loved to hear my father tell stories about his childhood. He was born in Russia, the youngest of eight children. Two of his brothers were close enough in age to share his childhood, but by the time he was five or six, the other five must have seemed more like surrogate parents—a fifteen-year-old brother, two sisters, eighteen and twenty, and two older brothers, twenty-three and twenty-six. His father emigrated to the United States when my father was an infant, and he didn't see him again until he was six years old; his father was a complete stranger when my father came to this country. During the intervening years, some of the older brothers and sisters had joined my grandfather in America. The last to come were my grandmother, my father, and his next oldest brother, then eight years old.

My grandmother was a baker. I loved to hear my father tell about how he would curl up to sleep on the warm stove in the cold Russian winter. I thought it was wonderful that there was a dirt floor and that the chickens were allowed into the house! For me the story of coming to America by boat in 1902 was full of romantic adventure because it was so utterly different from the life I knew. My father told me that to get to the boat they traveled by train from Russia to Holland. His mother brought along hardboiled eggs, bread, and a hard cheese cut in triangles, and in Holland she traded some of the eggs for oranges. They traveled steerage on the boat and my father was very seasick. But at some time when he was on the deck, some of the rich people on the upper decks threw pennies down to the poor immigrants, and my father caught some in his cap.

The boat landed in Hoboken, from whence the passengers would be taken to Ellis Island for processing. My grandmother and those uncles and aunts already living here hired a rowboat and rowed from Manhattan to New Jersey in order to welcome the new arrivals. They brought food with them, which the sailors brought up to the deck with ropes. My father had never seen a banana or a tomato before, and thought they were terrible.

Nine members of the family lived in a four-room tenement. There was one toilet in the hall for four families. As my father's brothers and sisters married and moved out, boarders were taken in. My father cannot recall ever having slept alone in a bed. He was sent to a special school to learn English for awhile, and then was placed in second grade in a public school. He always did very well in school, and while I concede he was very intelligent, I have the feeling that part of his high academic achievement was due to the fact that he was not sent to school until he was about seven years old! No pressures, no anxiety—lots of readiness!

A psychologist friend of ours who met my father many years ago was very intrigued by him. My father is a gentle, good human being, a truly ethical man. The psychologist wanted to give him a battery of personality tests in the hope that he could figure out what forces created "men of peace" like my father. My father and I were talking about his childhood as I began working on this chapter. His parents married (as total strangers) when his mother was sixteen, his father seventeen. With eight children, his mother never hit a child and never commanded or threatened. He remembers her (as I do) as the gentlest of souls. His father slapped him once, when he and his brother were giggling during an important religious ritual on one of the Jewish holidays. "I was so shocked," he told me. "He had never, ever done anything like that before, so I knew it was something very important." The struggle for survival was the core of life for every member of the family, and from the roots of that experience developed a sense of community, a clannishness. Even much later, when many of them became comfortably affluent, the family remained the center of their lives.

As a young child, I felt like an outsider. I suppose the fact that my father was the youngest and therefore most "Americanized" made it possible for him to move away from his family both geographically and emotionally. He became interested in a religious group radically different from the traditions of his own background—The Society for Ethical Culture, a group concerned with "rational humanism," an approach to life that emphasizes the cultivation of ethical relationships for human beings here on earth, without any preoccupation with ritual or traditional religious ceremonies or beliefs. He married a woman from a very different kind of background from his own, and as a young child I thought that in some ways we were superior to my father's family. The old religion was too primitive, the family ties too strong and constricting.

I learned much later, as an adult, how ambivalent I had felt. I really loved going to see my father's family. Although my grandparents could not speak English, I felt greatly loved. Unconditional love was served up generously by all the aunts with every course during the gigantic meals. And although my grandmother and I could never exchange a word, the look in her eyes when she would hand me some candy or nuts tied up in a handkerchief remains a palpably clear communication of great tenderness. I had a wonderful time on the rare occasions when I slept overnight at the house with all my cousins.

But I never allowed myself to enjoy it too much, then. While part of me was dying to hear my father's stories, and to be a member of this tight clan, another part of me was disdainful of foreign accents and old customs. Who needed a religion that was so *old?* We were rational, free, modern—American.

My father's family all built homes together in a summer colony. All except us—we went elsewhere. My father's family remained quite insular, for the most part; my life was less provincial, more cosmopolitan. In the long run I think I have had a more adventurous life than most of my paternal relatives, and I'm glad. But I learned a great deal from the examination of my mixed feelings. There was a part of me that wanted desperately to belong—to be at home in the clan, not to feel strange or superior. Loving was simpler; you belonged, you were loved because you were a member of the family. No conditions, no complications. There was a kind of all-encompassing earthiness, an instinctive humanity, that was most seductive.

I always had a deep sense of belonging with my mother's family. We saw each other all the time, and I felt greatly loved. The life style was more familiar—like our own. My memories are vivid and intense, a great consciousness of how different and special each relative was, and yet how we all blended into one.

My parents had an unusual number of close personal friends as well, and these all played a significant part in the cohesive, secure, loving setting of my growing up.

What I think I have learned is that young children desperately need a sense of clan, of belonging. Grade school-age children thrive best in a commune—an extended family setting. If these are the years for learning to relate as an individual in a group, it is comfortable to live in a laboratory where one can experiment! Preschool children need lots of individual attention; adolescents often need far more privacy than is possible in a communal setting. But from about six to twelve, it seems to me it would be helpful to children if we were to offer them a greater sense of family community.

It may seem cruel to suggest that children need an extended family when, for so many children who are being raised in single-parent families, the family has actually become more fragmented. I don't think this is an insurmountable problem. When schools focus on mutual help instead of competition, teachers will begin to be role models not unlike my aunts and uncles, permitting children to be cousins to one another instead of rivals. In addition, a family, a clan, doesn't have to take the old forms to be real or significant. Single parents can form into communities, families can rediscover the importance of being connected to other people, related or not. In recent years there have been a number of places in which older people and younger families have developed a system of "adopting" each other, when they live far away from their own relatives. In the cities and suburbs groups of parents are beginning to form cooperative services of all kinds. The development of a wide variety of types of communes has also indicated the needs of many adults and children for an extended family. Blood ties are irrelevant, we are discovering. People with common needs and purposes can provide each other with deep affection and support. Some years ago I went to visit a number of different kinds of communes. A group of young professional people had bought a city townhouse; it made possible a level of comfort they couldn't have afforded alone. A suburban commune was made up of four families joined by a need for cooperative child care; redoing an old mansion, they had made six self-contained apartments for privacy, but they shared the care of twelve young children. Another commune was close to a college campus and satisfied the needs of single students, a divorced mother, and several unmarried couples. Some communes are formed around a common religious or political philosophy, some around cooperative farming or crafts.

What I found was that they all suffered the imperfections of life anywhere, under any circumstances, but in many ways this seemed to me to be one reasonable, possible alternative for some people, and perhaps this may be most true for families with grade-school children.

More than anything else, I think school-age children

need principles to live by, a code of ethics to guide their experimentations in group living—and people who serve as role models by what they do. My relationship with my father seems to me to have become more important during the grade school years than earlier. He was a beacon; he led me through my first conscious struggles with "right" and "wrong." By some strange quirk of character, he really lives what he believes! He is a moral man, with a code of ethics that is in the marrow of his bones. It is a morality that is strict—and as time has gone by I have rejected parts of it that no longer suit me—but it was impossible not to be deeply influenced as a child. Some fathers get mean about goodness and badness—they smack you around if you're bad. My father spanked me only once during my entire childhood. I was about four; it was a cold night, and I had bronchitis. He caught me tiptoing barefoot in the hall, after having a bath. Characteristically, I was about to help myself to some chocolate peppermints on a hall table. He was concerned with my health, and I'm sure the spanking was a tap on the behind, but it was so out of character for him that I never forgot it—and have never let him forget it! He never hit my younger brother.

He is, in the most profound sense, "a good man," and so startlingly so, in this world of imperfect beings, that I think he taught me a great deal about what children need in their lives during the school-age years. I needed to know there were standards for me to try to live up to. I needed to know that there *were* some fundamental values about which there could be no doubt. Of these values, one was perfectly clear. *It is wrong for people to hurt each other*. At the core of my life, that is still the idea which motivates me.

Because he was a loving father, his influence was far greater than it might otherwise have been. If a parent is cruel, he makes it easy for you to reject him and even hate him. In my case I invested my father with magical powers. Where he was really a gentle and reasonable man, I took his standards as if they were being handed down by Cotton Mather as hellfire-and-brimstone commands. Later I was able to see his less earthshaking human dimensions, his fallibility. Then, I wanted him to be all powerful. I think children crave the nourishment of a strict code of ethics, which can later be modified. It was a philosophy of life to be used as background music in one's daily living. What it came down to fundamentally was my feeling that it was *necessary* to be a decent human being, to treat others as I wished to be treated.

I know that the standards he set for me have made it possible for me to feel proud of my work and my life because they have been in the service of better human relations. What I did not learn from him—and what I had to learn later, the hard way—was that being good to others has to start with oneself. I have become far better able to give to others in recent years as I began nourishing my own life more fully. But much of that profound sense of injustice remains, and I'm not sorry. Whenever I am in a fury at some outrage against human beings, I know the roots of this necessary social feeling began when I was six or seven or eight, when I was becoming aware of the fact that my father was a good person and expected the same of me.

At the time when my daughter was growing up, we put great emphasis on the importance of peer relationships. It was a natural consequence of the awareness of the fact that during the years from six to twelve children needed to begin the socialization process. But I think now that we really went overboard. In the first stages of learning how to live in a community of others, children are too insecure —too uncivilized—to be guided by their own instincts. They need supervision, direction, group experiences that include imposed external adult values.

Many of us as parents in the 1950s and early 1960s were overly concerned with our children's "being popular." We frequently permitted activities of which we didn't really approve. For example, I thought it was ridiculous for eleven-year-olds to go to social dancing classes, but I gave in because Wendy acted as if she would become a social outcast if I refused to let her go.

Many of the demands for group conformity are really a child's cry for limits, a hunger to be nourished with good standards. The trouble is that we begin to believe a child who screams, "You'll ruin my life! Nobody will ever be my friend!" We weaken—and in that weakening, we permit the child to believe that people really are judged by how much they conform.

The struggle for independence is so important in adolescence that one has to allow children greater room for experimentation, but grade school children should have a clear and comforting feeling that parents are still in charge. They may yell—they will finally rebel later on, against some of our expectations, and a good thing—but this is a time to be firm about things that matter. As I look back now, I am sure that our daughter was happiest when we stuck to our convictions and did not give in too easily.

There was one episode that indicated this so clearly to both my husband and myself. He had forbidden Wendy to watch a certain television program because he felt it had a quality of ugly sadism that, on moral grounds, he detested. She fought him tooth and nail, screaming that she was the only child in her class who couldn't watch. One night, when she was sleeping at a friend's house, she called and asked special permission to watch it. My husband said she could watch this once, and when he hung up he looked bewildered; how would we have known if she'd just watched it? She wanted standards, no matter how she yelled.

We need to live righteously, by a code of ethics we practice as well as preach, if we want our children to do likewise, and we need to have the thick skin and the guts to stand by our principles no matter how mad the children get. That's moral nutrition at the age they need it most.

Such parenting must be done by all adults in and outside the family. Children spend a great deal of time in school, and when they are taught that the only thing that matters is beating someone else at whatever it is you are doing, there can never be a real sense of what cooperation means.

If I were in charge of the world, every single day in every classroom, everywhere, children would be living cooperatively and learning what it means to be a responsible citizen in a democracy. No child would ever be considered ready for high school—or whatever better equivalent we invent for education beyond sixth grade—until he or she had directly participated in serving community needs. Every class would have an opportunity to develop its own projects for finding out what is needed and doing something about it—cleaning up an empty lot in the neighborhood, planting flowers at a shopping center, getting the garbage out of the river, collecting books for children who don't have any, taking cookies made in cooking class to a senior citizen's club.

It seems no accident to me that violence and crime are increasing among children. They are reflecting the immorality of the adult society, and their pain over the social neglect involved. There is no clearer example of this than the issue of integration of schools and neighborhoods. It seems to have remained an abstract ethical principle that in a democracy every person matters—has equal rights of opportunity. Surely the moral crisis in this country about school integration does more to damage decent human relations in the elementary school than anything within the children themselves. The failure of successful busing is, as far as I am concerned, an obscenity, an immorality far beyond any childish cruelty ever invented by a street gang. What we tell our children every day of their lives is that some people are better than others. The hierarchy of better and worse varies from family to family. In some families children of divorce are dangerous. Children who live in communes, whose parents are unmarried, or who, God forbid, have homosexual parents, are not fit playmates in the back yard. Children who are black or speak Spanish are also dangerous, and too different to be tolerated. All smart, white, middle-class children from solid, straight families ought to be huddled together, so as not to be contaminated by inferior people.

Parents are far more guilty for the prejudices of children than the schools—many of which have tried to experiment with heterogenous groupings. What they find in classes where children are *not* separated by test and achievement scores, or other divisive categories, is that *all* the children ultimately benefit. Mental health is catching. Children who are more privileged, and usually also overprotected, learn to be more self-reliant, more spontaneous. Children who have had fewer experiences in learning, more emotional trauma, begin to flower in a loving, accepting, stimulating environment.

There is one catch—you need parents and teachers who really believe that in the long run democracy works; that differences enrich, not hurt; that nobody is really any better or more worthwhile than anyone else. Such experiments rarely are allowed to go on; sooner more often than later parents demand that their children be put back into smart and dumb groups—euphimistically labeled "fast and slow tracks." The parents of the "good students" don't want their children held back; the parents of the "slower learners" want their children to get extra help and not be lost in the crowd. We adults create the environment that is most antithetical to compassionate sharing and mutual concern and respect of all people for each other—and then we wonder why democracy stumbles.

There *is* another alternative—small classes with teaching aides to assist so that each child can pursue his own interests and develop the skills he wants at his own pace, sharing his learning with others, experiencing the special and unique characteristics of everyone else around him. There *are* such schools. None of them work perfectly; all have many problems in working out the details of how individual growth and group living can reinforce and enhance each other. But I have never, ever, run across a school that was at least *trying* to live up to such noble goals that wasn't helping its children develop the kinds of social values desperately needed in a democratic society.

These are the most impressionable years for the development of attitudes toward others, for the enjoyment or the fear of differences, for pleasure in or prejudice against sharing life with the variety of people around one. When adults indicate that there are enormous advantages and adventures in being with different kinds of people, we might begin to hope for a society that did not reject its individual members for color or background or religion or family life style, but rather celebrated whatever special enrichment each person can add to the whole. Nobody ever learned to be a responsible, self-directed, cooperating citizen of a democratic society without the help of just those kinds of grownups.

The problems we face today are so crucial, so complex —so dangerous—that we desperately need a new kind of citizenry. We cannot tolerate individual enterprise as we have known it, because it has come to mean, "I can do as I please," even if that means polluting the air and the water, destroying crops while people starve, building monstrous skyscrapers and highways when human beings need places to live. The social good must supercede individual power and affluence or no one will survive. There must be a complete reordering of priorities. The question is, can we do that and still allow for individual differences? I think we can; there were experiences in my life where that was proven to be true. And most of all during adolescence and early adulthood.

Chapter 4

Like my grandmother, I was diary prone. In her case there were only a few torn and yellowed fragments left; the record of my adolescence is so voluminous and well-preserved that I find it impossible to select a representative portion to include!

I started it in 1939. On the cover, along with my name, it says: "From aged 16 and 8 months to 17 and 7 months. Story of a typical adolescent existence—ideas, experiences, problems, etc. To be published in book form not early [*sic*] than 1950." I suppose I must have considered twenty-seven so far past my prime that it would no longer matter what dark secrets were revealed!

I'm twenty-five years late already, but while I feel slightly guilty about not publishing that diary as instructed, the sad irony is that I now find it very tame indeed. I knew very little about the secret self beneath the facade. The diary is jam-packed with activity. I seemed to have constant dates with friends, although I bemoaned my fate for being "left out" so much. I was at dead center of never less than ten of the romantic intrigues current at any given time; my life at school sounds fascinating and stimulating—even while I write of the tortures of tests and grades. I was madly in love with four male teachers, was reading five to ten books a month, going to movies and plays every weekend. My parents must have been very generous about an allowance, because in addition to such entertainments, I seemed to be eating out a great deal. Of course things were different then; at one point I described such an outing: ". . . We tried a fabulous new French Restaurant which was quite expensive, but we did get a whole meal for 75¢ and it was delicious."

I was very aware of political issues, horrified by the war in Europe, desperately trying to hang on to my inherent pacifism. "If war comes, I guess I'll just die of misery," I wrote.

I'm sure it will come as a great surprise to my readers that I tended toward the dramatic! I was always in agony or ecstasy, and the shifts back and forth could occur five times a day. But these mood swings were related to real, everyday events—did I or did I not get invited to a party, did or did not a certain boy call me, did I or did I not do well in class.

I wrote consistently about how wonderful my parents were to me; despite the ups and downs, it was clearly a very happy, productive, busy life I led, full of loving friends and relatives. Every word of it is true—but like my mother's letters during my infancy, it represents half the truth.

It is the other half about which I've never written, and which seems to me to offer some useful clues about the unique and essential tasks of adolescence—the hidden river of my inner life revealed long after 1950 in my search for myself.

It is very difficult for me to write about these later insights. It is impossible for me to examine my own adolescence dispassionately. My only real regret in life is that I didn't make more mistakes, and adolescence is the time for that to begin. Although my diary now seems to me charming and ebullient and full of lively experiences, I was safe and secure, with no risks; I never lived dangerously.

The first time I ever went to see a therapist, when I was in my mid-twenties, I started out by saying, "I don't understand how I could have any problems—I had perfect parents." That was about thirty years ago. What I think I have learned in these intervening years is that "good parents" may interfere with the necessary developmental tasks of adolescence unless they consciously and deliberately *let go*.

By the time *My Fair Lady* appeared on Broadway, I had had several years of intensive psychotherapy. I bought the record, and the first time I played it was on an evening when I was home alone. When "I Could Have Danced All Night" began, I suddenly burst into tears; I sobbed as if my heart would break; I was in mourning for a part of adolescence I had never had. I had now gone beyond my initial resistance to examining my life and was beginning to understand that while it was true that my parents were good people who loved me greatly, it was also true that when it was time for me to begin to try my own wings— to rebel and leave *their* nest for the further discovering of my own life, they were overprotective; by their loving concern and subtle controls they seduced me into remaining A Good Child. I had never "danced all night."

It seems to me now that adolescence must be a time to begin to discover one's own most authentic gifts and needs, and in that process one must take chances—insist on the right to begin the lifetime task of self-actualization. This can only begin to be achieved in a climate of daring, and left pretty much to their own devices, most teen-agers know this instinctively.

I did not yet understand this when my own daughter became a teen-ager. I was as anxious and overcontrolling as my parents had been with me. I had somewhat more flexible attitudes, but I really didn't trust myself or my child. Times had changed, however—to understate it considerably—and Wendy and her peers were children of a social and sexual revolution. While it was painful for Wendy to fight us because we, too, were trying hard to be "good parents," full of understanding—and controlling— demands, she did rebel and escape. How glad I am, now that I have begun to understand my own long-delayed growing up.

When Wendy was about twenty-three, I asked her one day how come she had been able to be so much more open and loving, and uninhibited, with a mother who had been so rigid and puritanical. Her answer was wonderful; she said, "I never listened to what you *said;* I listened to your *feelings.*"

Recently my father was visiting me at Cape Cod. At dinner one night, talking with a group about education, he commented quite casually, "Eda should have gotten her Ph.D. She should still do it." I felt an irrational, overwhelming rage rising inside of me. I felt I was suddenly in the midst of a dangerous war, and that I must attack immediately or I would be lost. In a nasty, mean tone of voice I yelled at the poor man, *"I'd rather be dead!"* He looked startled and chagrined, and later, after dinner, said, "I guess the reason Mother and I always felt so strongly about your getting your degrees was because of Mother's heartache over not having finished her own schooling."

Why had I gotten so upset? Trying to examine it, I thought to myself, My God, I'm *fifty-three* years old, and I decided a long time ago that I wanted to be a writer now, not a psychologist. My father has no omnipotent control over my decisions. Ah, but once he did—and I still haven't gotten over it. Now I can reassure myself; my father is a good man with strong opinions. He and my mother often wanted things for me that I might very well have not wanted for myself, if I had had the ability to explore and to choose; I know that now, and it is childish to get angry. But I understand the fear and the defensiveness, because when I was young and I might have been making those explorations, I was listening and obeying instead. It still makes me angry—at myself—that I didn't have the courage to find my own way. There is still a residue of guilt beneath the rage—what a naïve, sappy, scared kid I was.

Many years ago my husband explained to me the meaning of "ontological guilt." He told me it was the very worst kind. It means feeling guilty because one is not living one's own life, fulfilling one's own potentials. As the years have passed I have come to understand this more deeply, and it accounts for my awful sensitivity about examining my own adolescence; I have too much ontological guilt.

The problem is that no matter how much one learns about human fallibility, compassion and acceptance are still hard to come by. When I became deeply depressed at the prospect of having to write this chapter, I said to Larry, "I can't forgive myself for the fact that I was a coward; that I didn't have the guts to fight harder to become free, when that's what I should have been doing." His answer was, "You have nothing to forgive yourself for. You were a *nice person*—decent and brave—and you couldn't bear to hurt your parents when you knew how much they loved you. You made a sacrifice which you later discovered had cost you too much—but it was done out of tenderness, and you have had the courage to fight for your own growth ever since." Well, then, my irrational mind stumbles along, if I mustn't blame myself, shall I blame my parents?

Equally nonsensical, unfair—and useless. My parents never for one moment *ever* meant to hurt me in any way. What happened was from good intentions only.

My father had strong opinions and ethical values. He spoke wisely and gently. He never yelled and he never really punished. It was impossible (for me) not to believe that he must know what was best. My mother was a mixture of Victorian and liberated woman. In addition to unconscious feelings of unworthiness, she had been raised in a Victorian household as far as sexual mores and manners were concerned. A great-aunt who grew up in the same household told me that, into her twenties, she still believed you could get pregnant by kissing! Sexual repression, rigid and inflexible rules about what was appropriate before marriage, had been deeply ingrained, and coupled with those feelings of unworthiness, my mother—despite the genuine liberation of her career—was a very old-fashioned girl when it came to relations between the sexes.

She was a great letter writer, and I saved many of her letters. From when I was twelve until I turned twenty-one she wrote me literally hundreds of letters—all single spaced, often at least three to four pages long—although we were living under the same roof! They were mostly exhortations to make myself more attractive to boys. But they were also subtle messages about the desirability for postponing sexuality until marriage, and since, at the deepest level of my unconscious, I knew the terrible secret of my sensuous yearnings, the only choice seemed to me to be to avoid temptation.

I succeeded quite well! I fell in and out of love with boys who were at least as sexually repressed as I was. I developed intense friendships with girls and platonic friendships with boys. I became far more strait-laced than my parents. I was using up so much psychic energy to avoid dealing with my emerging passionate propensities that I managed to develop various psychosomatic disorders with which to occupy my mind, and my inability to concentrate and focus my attention meant that I was constantly having difficulty with more precise school subjects such as math and French grammar, so that I could keep myself preoccupied with the ever-present danger of failure.

The thing was, I was talented enough to succeed very well, even at being neurotic!

Excerpts from a couple of my mother's letters indicate what almost all of them were about. The first of these samples appeared under my door one morning, after I had stated the night before at dinner that I hated everybody and would not go to any more social gatherings!

> . . . You have so many fine qualities of mind and heart —what in the world is wrong? Only something in your attitude and behavior, not in yourself. I don't want to lecture. I only want to help you. It is nonsensical to give up going to groups. You have met boys through clubs and school. Where did Marian meet Fred? At a meeting she went to with a friend. Where did Evelyn meet Harold? At a dinner party. Sidney and Anita met at a resort. Dad and I met through

our work—another kind of group experience. Betty met Charlie at church; Sue met Henry at a picnic. . . . The first thing to remember is that circulation broadens one's experiences. That's just step one. After that comes such things as poise, self confidence, and friendliness. You are almost antagonistic sometimes, instead of friendly and outgoing. No one who starts out with a chip on her shoulder gets very far. And it doesn't hurt to exercise a little "female charm." I don't want you to be self conscious, but that you stop acting indifferent, that you go to groups and circulate. Don't make up your mind so quickly about everybody. Your critical attitude shows in your face. I'm sure you will marry someday; all I want is for you to establish right attitudes and sensible behavior for yourself now and not cheat yourself out of the fun and friendships of a well-rounded social life. You will make a wonderful mother some day and you will have to recognize that women must "get their men," not in a vulgar sense but using their "God-given" powers to good advantage and not pretend indifference. . . .

I despised dancing classes, held in the school gym. I was an A-number-one wallflower. On one occasion, when my ego was especially bruised, I bought myself a big box of Whitman's chocolates at our neighborhood drugstore, and when I got home I told my parents a boy I had a crush on had bought it for me. They were a little surprised, but I would have gotten away with my crime except for one small detail. I didn't have enough money with me, so I charged the candy to my parents' monthly account and "forgot" to pay it as I'd planned to, the next day. It appeared on their next bill. I'm sure that unconsciously I wanted to be found out and my suffering at the dance classes alleviated. I was not punished for lying; my parents were very understanding. But another letter appeared:

> ... I know you are very upset about the dancing class. It is not terribly important; life has its ups and downs. However, the important thing, as I see it, is—are you going to take such "failures" lying down? Or are you going to seek to make them at least partial successes by virtue of your own sense, understanding and efforts? Let's say, merely for the sake of argument and not at all because this will necessarily prove to be true, that you are not ever going to be a "hit" as a social butterfly. You know you are *fortunate* in having other truly compensating assets in other fields to give you joy and satisfaction and recognition and to make people like to be near you. But to say you intend to quit dancing school is to be stupidly unwilling to face real needs and to do your best. ... Are you going to be unequipped and unfamiliar with the social skills befitting such occasions? What an utter fool you would be—unless you plan to go into a nunnery! On the contrary, if I were you I would resolve with all my might to make the most of the possibilities I have and can acquire. I would say to myself, "I will master this

thing. I won't necessarily become the Belle of the Ball but I'll equip myself as best I can to function at my maximum powers. I'll be pleasant and sociable and friendly. I'll care loads about my appearance and cleanliness and skin and good taste generally. I will learn to be an inviting personality. I will be glad for whatever I do achieve. I will realize that I can achieve greater successes at things in which I am more talented by nature—writing, acting, etc. . . . By means of courage and perseverance I will function as nearly 100% as I possibly can." Runaway behavior is cowardly, isn't it? Many truly afflicted people—blind or lame or deaf . . . have conquered even these sad obstacles and have made something of themselves. I would hate to see you do less. . . .

My poor mother! How constricted her own adolescence must have been—how awful and rigid the "shoulds." It was not easy for me to include even this much of my mother's letters. I miss her greatly, and had the feeling she would not have liked what I was writing. Two days after I had written the above lines about my "poor mother," my father, knowing I planned to include autobiographical material in this book, sent me a letter he had found, written by my mother in 1906 when she was eleven years old, to her father and stepmother (recently married). Here is the letter:

Dear Parents,
Please excuse me for my terrible conduct. I didn't mean it. I am going to practice real hard if you give

me another chance. I will also try to be good to you both.

From your loving child
Jeannette

I wept as I read it. Such a terrible striving to be "good." How my mother must have been struggling with mixed feelings about this second marriage. One generation after another—feeling guilty! Her terrible "crime" was probably not practicing the piano and maybe "talking back." I was so glad to get the letter, for it was like a message that I ought to use whatever I need of my past in the cause of doing whatever I can to help free younger people from some of their chains. I know my mother would want that, too.

I invited disastrous social events and begged for punishment, in order to keep my volatile and passionate nature safely repressed. There was one period when a girl I had met at summer camp and I started a salacious correspondence, full of dirty jokes and indecent drawings—as shocking as a woman's *breast*—imagine! One of my letters was intercepted by the other girl's mother and sent on to the camp director, who called my mother. I was mortified when confronted with the evidence. We had a conference —the director, my mother, and I. It was agreed that the other mother was unenlightened; my own mother and the camp director understood that "young people go through such phases." But it was a silly thing to have done; after all, I knew all the facts of sex and understood how beautiful it could be when one grew up and got married. Looking back, I think I must have wished, at some unconscious level, that instead of being so charming and understanding, the ladies would beat me or send me to my room for a week's imprisonment. What I have since discovered is that those of my contemporaries who were having much more fun than I was tended to be in a constant state of anger at their parents, or feeling thoroughly misunderstood—freeing them to do as they pleased!

The psychological messages I picked up as a teen-ager were that I should be attractive and charming and popular —but never lose control. That I was gifted with many abilities and talents, but I should choose a career that would give me security. Until my mother's death, when I was in my late forties and obviously had made a success of my career-life—and no one enjoyed this more than she did—she was still expressing regrets that I hadn't become a public school teacher so I would have a pension, like that cousin who had skipped second grade and who was still being held up as an example!

If I had fought harder, I know my parents would have stood by me, no matter what; that knowledge is the source of my ontological guilt. But they certainly didn't make it easy to fight; they were so reasonable and nice and loving! The problem was that while I was a nice person, loved my parents, and didn't want to hurt them, I was not really passive and easy going. At a deep, unconscious level (I knew nothing at all about it at the time) I was a passionate, poetic, divinely discontented soul, yearning to be free.

The adolescence I actually *lived* might well have been too tempestuous for some; for others it might have been just right. What I have since learned about myself is that I was terrified of the restless adventurer within, and to quell that terror I clipped my own wings.

During the early years of psychotherapy, as I began to search for my "true nature," I had a dream in which my therapist became a baton twirler at the head of a parade. She was wearing a slinky, tight-fitting gold lamé dress and a dark satin cape. Her movements were so sexually provocative that I, marching behind her, wanted desperately to leave the parade, I was so ashamed and embarrassed, but I seemed unable to do so. At one point her gyrations became so wild that her cape flew open and I saw that the lining was bright red.

In real life the therapist was indeed an adorable, sexy French lady. The week before the dream I had seen a marvelous play with Jessica Tandy and Hume Cronyn— Sidney Kingsley's *Madam Will You Walk,* in which Hume Cronyn played the devil in disguise. The only way you were supposed to know the truth was the red lining of his cape. My therapist laughed as we discussed the dream. "I see you have made *me* the devil," she said. "Instead of marching behind me, and making it appear that I am leading you into a life of depravity and sinfulness, perhaps it is time you realized that you would like to be that lady in the gold dress, making all those gyrations!" That was the beginning of the rediscovery of a buried self.

When I was a child it was not too unusual for an eleven-year-old still to be playing with dolls. I had a "Madame Alexander" doll called "Bubbles," and she was very life-like. She was about the size of a year-old child. I lived on the eleventh floor of an apartment house, and each window had a guard rail. I used to put blankets and pillows out on the window ledge within the guard rail, so that "Bubbles" could have an airing when I didn't actually take her out to the park in her carriage.

In the spring of my eleventh year, I got up very early one morning and decided to give Bubbles an airing. As I began to arrange her on the pillow on the window sill, I looked down on a building that was only about six stories high and immediately next to my apartment house. I was startled to see two young people in passionate embrace against one side of the open roof. My first reaction was one of shock and shyness; I was an intruder, and it seemed to me I should bring my doll in, close the window, and pull down the shade. But I was too fascinated. Instead, I merely drew back so that I could not be seen, and I watched.

They seemed very grown up to me at the time, but I suppose they were teen-agers. He was dark skinned and had beautiful, wavy, shiny black hair—he looked Spanish or Italian. The girl was taller, very fair, with the reddest hair I'd ever seen. There was such a quality of urgency and tension about the way they held each other that I sensed this was a secret tryst and that no one else knew they were meeting there.

I had had crushes on boys in school since first grade, and my parents were avant-garde for those days, so I knew about sex. In my head. But this was different. I think what happened to me at that window was the awakening to passion, and it both fascinated and terrified me.

That first day the young lovers clung to each other for a few minutes and then each left separately. The gesture that moved and excited me the most was when the boy swept her red hair up in his hands and began to kiss her neck. I looked away and fussed with my doll, but that night when I went to bed, all I could envision was that kissing.

I watched every day for their return—poor Bubbles was given the air in all kinds of weather so that I could legitimatize my window watching in case anyone asked me what I was doing. Their visits to the roof were infrequent—perhaps once or twice a week—but as time went on the love-making became more intense, and I am sure, looking back now, more than forty years later, that in some profound way this was a time of crisis, a shifting for me from childhood to puberty. I became increasingly preoccupied with the lovers, thought about them a great deal, fantasied myself in place of the girl, and was more and more disturbed and excited by what I saw and remembered vividly.

It was during this period that I began to relinquish playing with dolls. On one occasion, in Morningside Park, someone ridiculed me. I heard two boys laughing at me—"Look at that big kid playing with dolls." I had one friend with whom I'd been playing with dolls since the age of four, and we often visited each other with our dolls. I remember one Saturday taking my doll on the Fifth Avenue bus to her house, and feeling again that people were laughing at me. That day I told her about the young lovers on the roof, but she seemed uninterested. Our friendship was never the same, and that was the last day I recall taking that doll out in public. She sat on a shelf in my room for a long time, but there was no more pretending to feed her or put her to sleep—or sit her on the window ledge. Once more, several weeks later, the lovers appeared. It was now summer, and it was about six o'clock in the morning. I'd gotten up to go to the bathroom, and automatically looked out as I had for weeks, without seeing them. This time it seemed they might have been there all night. They were lying on a blanket, and as I watched, unable to move or look away, I realized that they were having intercourse. I became frightened, and ran back to bed. I never looked out the window early in the morning again. But I was totally preoccupied with a kind of pure sensuality. I tried desperately to forget. It was bothering me as nothing had ever bothered me before.

Some time later (I was now twelve), I was lying in the back of our family car returning from a Sunday visit to my father's relatives in Brooklyn. I noticed that my wrists and ankles ached, and thought it was just the fatigue from a long day and getting to bed late. My mother took my temperature when we got home and it was slightly elevated. By the next morning I felt fine, and my temperature was normal. However, during the afternoon, in school, I began to have an aching feeling in my arms and legs again, and when I got home, I again had a slight fever.

When this pattern continued for several more days, my mother took me to the doctor. I don't remember how soon the diagnosis was made, but when I was finally told that I had rheumatic fever and would have to stay in bed for several months, I recall thinking it was the end of the world. I remember riding home on the top deck of an open bus, looking up at the stars and wondering if I would ever come back to the world—and while dramatizing this to the fullest, I know now, looking back, that I also felt some sense of relief—as if some major decision was being postponed and that I was safe from some great danger, for the time being.

The long period of inactivity that ensued, accompanied by the gradual onset of puberty, affected me physically as well as psychologically. It reinforced tendencies already established. I gained weight and became clumsier, I lost touch with my classmates. When I returned to school I felt like an outsider. At the time, and for many years thereafter, I thought that my feelings of ineptitude, my lack of self-confidence with boys, were at least in part due to my illness and its aftermath of overweight and physical awkwardness. I have since come to understand that this hiatus was a time in which I unconsciously concluded that I was faced with an either-or decision; either I would turn into a fallen woman—a whore with no morals or self-control—or if I wanted to be a good girl, I must do everything possible to avoid being sexually provocative. I conveniently "forgot" my rooftop lovers and did not regain the memory until I was in my early thirties. It never showed enough to really worry anybody. I managed to stay just fat enough to insulate myself against most dangers; I became increasingly successful in a broad range of school activities—one of the first girls to be nominated for Student Council president, editor of the literary magazine, star of school plays. I became, God help me, "A Wonderful Person with High Ideals."

Every once in a while some perceptive young man would come along and sense the smoldering cauldron beneath that plump and sanctimonious facade. When I was fifteen or sixteen, I went with my family for a vacation to a resort in the Adirondacks. I was an excellent swimmer, loved boating, and spent a good deal of time at the beach. There was a tall, dark, handsome lifeguard (naturally!) and I "fell in love," which meant I flirted and fantasied. I was astonished and uneasy, as well as terribly flattered, when he seemed responsive. (My God, there were all those beautiful, sexy, *thin* women around—how come he seemed to like me?) One day, when I started to go off alone in a canoe, he said he was going off duty and would like to take me for a ride. It soon became clear he had more in mind than that, but before I allowed myself time to explore my own real feelings (heaven forbid!), I was giving him a long, serious lecture on the nature of true love, and why I was waiting for marriage. It was a recitation of my mother's letters, and it sure stopped him cold! I think that was the first time he'd been defeated on the territory of oratory. When my family and I left a few days later, he was standing outside the resort office. He kissed me tenderly on the forehead and said, "You remind me of my mother."

It was a crushing insult, but as we drove away, and I could return to the security of fantasy, I felt a sense of relief; I was quite pleased with myself.

Since then, that and other similar situations (the bohemian with the loft in Greenwich Village, the socialist who explained the political dimensions of free love—who may sound like stereotypes but were real!) have returned to haunt me. What if I hadn't been such a prig and a prude? . . . Disastrous and painful episodes, perhaps—maybe not. One thing for sure—I would have learned more about myself, and if pleasure had been part of that risk taking, that unconditional giving would have taught me something of value; the more one searches for one's own needs and the more one dares to fulfill them—the more one can love and be loved.

Certainly the implications of these memories go far beyond the issue of sensuality. They symbolized a more general hunger for adventure, to be more daring, to respond to life less carefully and more spontaneously. It never occurred to me, consciously, that I might run away and become a writer or an actress; that I might refuse to go to college and write poetry in Paris; that I might choose a career that wasn't as respectable and secure as that of a teacher or child psychologist.

What I think I have learned from exploring the difference between what I was doing and experiencing, and the deeper and more authentic needs I was repressing, is that the adolescent years are a perfect setting for learning about what it means to live a *synergistic life*—and adults frequently spend all their energies trying to interfere with this essential process.

Thus far I have suggested that the earliest years of childhood give us a beginning sense of our individual uniqueness and the middle years awaken us to the demands as well as the satisfactions of belonging to a group. Human history is really all about the ways in which people have tried to reconcile their individual and social needs. In trying to explore what makes for a peaceful and productive society, anthropologist Ruth Benedict used the term "synergistic" to describe a culture in which individual fulfillment was viewed as an essential social good for all. She found that when human beings felt not only free but encouraged to develop and use their fullest potentials, community life flourished. I have learned nothing in all my years of searching and growing that makes more sense to me. On a personal level, I know beyond any doubt that the more I use whatever gifts I have, the more I become most truly myself—the more love and compassion I feel for everyone else. I want all other human beings to have what I have; out of my pleasure in selfhood, my capacity to love grows and grows.

Teen-agers have terrible worries and fears. They are devastated by the bodily changes taking place; they don't know who they are or who they will become. Their uncertainty, lack of self-confidence, sense of turmoil leave them shakingly vulnerable. They are shy, self-conscious, aching with longings, wanting desperately to become adults but terrified of what that means. What a marvelous moment for testing oneself, exploring new possibilities—making the necessary mistakes that teach us the most about ourselves and other people! Left to their own devices, what a glorious mess they would probably make of their lives—but what a lot they would learn!

Instead, the tendency of parents and educators has been to circumscribe the lives of teen-agers with great rigidity. When I was growing up this made some sense—and was inevitable, anyway. Social change came more slowly then, but even we had ten times as much freedom as our parents were likely to have had—and a hundred times more than our grandparents. Attitudes toward the sexual maturation of young people were necessarily wary and prohibitive, since birth control and abortion were illegal, dangerous, and not fit topics for people to talk about openly. Education for the most part was firmly locked into traditions that may have been appropriate in the 1800s, but had little to do with the twentieth century.

I seems to me that in today's world we might make a daring experiment. Suppose we were to use the shook-up nature of adolescence as fallow soil for the teaching of the meaning of a synergistic life? Might we be able—even in one or two generations— to create a population of young people who have come through the fires of self-discovery to such a degree that they understand in their guts what it means to be fully oneself as well as a cooperating world citizen?

A candid look at the state of the world suggests to me

that we have nothing to lose, and that almost any innovations would be an improvement on what we currently offer our young people.

If I were the parent of an adolescent today and had the power to create such a new environment for young people, I would certainly do it. Instead of trying to block off the turmoil of growth taking place, I would try to free it. Never again in our lives are we ever as open and daring as we might be in adolescence, if this was encouraged. Teenagers want more than anything else to take risks. There are some that we must prohibit—such as driving too fast or destroying their brains with amphetamines. But I suspect there would be fewer of those sorts of dangerous experiments if we were to allow genuine and productive adventures.

In most cases there is an unnecessary war between adults and adolescents. Unnecessary, but inevitable, considering what we do. There they are, with all that energy, that awakening sensuality, curious, sassy, confused, shy and bold, scared and defiant, wallowing in feelings of inferiority one minute and ready to dare anything the next. And what do we do with all those essentials for growing? We shut our young people up in boxes called "classrooms"; we tell them what they must study; we focus their attention on some dim future, showing no respect at all for the present, which is what matters to them most. Instead of offering the richest possible smorgasbord of learning experiences, every student has to take the same subjects—until, suddenly, at about eighteen, we demand to know what they have decided to spend the rest of their lives doing.

We pit them against each other even more than we did in grade school. The hierarchy of what represents success and failure is sharper, more clearly defined—just at the time that they begin to sense the richness of their differences. The more aware we are of their awakening sex drives, the more we encourage them to see their relationships as fraught with potential danger; we make them wary, self-conscious. In order to avoid the complications involved, we foster war, not love, between girls and boys. Since we are so afraid of sexual encounters during adolescence (mostly the residue of a different time in a different world), we struggle to restrict young people from viewing films or reading magazines that are explicitly sexual, but appear to have no qualms at all about allowing young people to see movies like *Clockwork Orange* or *Deliverance*. We end up with young people who dare not share their real feelings with each other and who rebel against the most ridiculous and inconsequential things (curfew, wearing apparel, profanity at the dinner table) because we have successfully constricted their lives.

The most daring pay no attention to us. But lying and secretiveness are a terrible price to pay in human relationships. Those who ignore adult demands the most tend to be those who feel the least loved—have the least to lose—and their experimentation is necessarily tainted by their self-hatred.

Many years ago a niece came to visit us. She had not seen

us very often, and expected us to be "real squares." Because she was about eighteen (and because it's always easier with someone else's child!), my husband gave her the following instructions for her stay in New York. First of all he told her, "If Eda and I have learned anything, it is that you only regret the things you don't do. The things that you do which turn out to be mistakes teach you a great deal—but you always regret the chances you didn't take." Our niece looked ready to faint; *this* from an *uncle*? He confounded her further by adding, "And another good rule is always try everything twice."

If our daughter were fifteen or sixteen again, I hope I would have the courage to tell her the same thing. I hope that I would trust what we had done those first fifteen years—that I would believe in the fundamental soundness and decency of my child. I would ask if I could be helpful in the matter of selecting a gynecologist with whom she could discuss birth control procedures and the hazards and safety measures involved in such matters as venereal disease and abortion, when *she* decided she might need such information. I hope I would encourage her to defy the traditional demands of the educational system, and once she had fulfilled the minimal legal requirement of attending school until the age of sixteen, to explore herself and her future by working, traveling, taking courses in any subjects that interested her. I know now that once she began to hone in on her own special needs and gifts, she would have the necessary motivation to obtain whatever required subjects and degrees she might decide she needed.

I no longer feel that I would be abdicating from responsibility or allowing my child to flounder in a sea of terrifying uncertainty. I would always be available for consultation—but far more important than that, I would make it absolutely clear that my new perception of what it means to be a loving and responsible parent of a teen-ager is that I would always be *there* to help pick up the pieces when she made the inevitable and necessary mistakes this kind of adventurous growing entails. And although the self-control might practically *kill* me, I would try my damnedest not to write any letters full of my expectations!

When Wendy did get into difficulties as a teen-ager, my reaction was always "What did I do wrong?" I was so caught up in the egocentricity of my delusions of omnipotence, that I rarely took the time to really look at my child, ask what it meant to her—what she was feeling and learning.

A few years ago, while I was working on a book for teen-agers,* I asked that same niece, now a teacher on the West Coast, to have some informal discussions with her junior high school students about their feelings about themselves, about growing up, about friends, parents, sex, love, and so on. She wrote me that her attempts had failed miserably; every student needed to defend him or herself against showing any vulnerability. Everything was just fine with everybody. She then resorted to having each student write me an unsigned letter or an anonymous composition on some aspect of adolescence. What poured out was anx-

* *You And Your Feelings,* (New York: Macmillan, 1975).

iety, pain, frustration, anger, and confusion; behind the façade of most of the youngsters in her class was genuine suffering. That seems to me to explain the competitiveness and self-consciousness of social relations during the teen years. Nobody is having a good time being him- or herself, so everybody is suspicious, shy, defensive, full of bravado; ganging up on each other becomes the only comfort—temporarily—until it is one's own turn to become the scapegoat.

As I look back at my intense feelings of unworthiness during adolescence, I realize they were the end product of trying to repress too much of my own nature. I came through those years safe and unscarred—but knowing little about who I really was. The price was too high—not only for myself but for others I cared about. Afraid to allow myself too much genuine fulfillment, my giving—my loving—remained conditional well into middle age.

That silly, stupid issue of the dancing class is a case in point. The lesson to be learned, as far as I am concerned, is that when I was a flop at dancing school and hated it, I ought to have been told it was ridiculous to try to do something that I didn't enjoy. If I had felt that it was far more sensible and appropriate to go hide in a closet and write some poetry or a play, or take a walk alone or go to a movie, the pleasure I would have taken in being myself and doing my own thing would inevitably have led to whatever kinds of social relationships I ultimately wanted to have. Of course, there was no way my mother could have known (any more than I did then) that the slightest crack in the wall—any act of pure "selfish" impulse—meant the danger of a life of total decadence and hedonism as far as I was concerned! It was clearly a case of all or nothing at all. I did not understand that even if one is consciously aware of one's real feelings, one still has choices—options. It never occurred to me that being a decent, sensitive, responsible sort, I might very well have made wise decisions most of the time—and that when I didn't, I would have learned from my mistakes.

Some months ago I was invited to a very soigné affair— a reception for a world-famous musician. It was a cocktail party at one of the fanciest hotels in New York, and I knew that all sorts of fascinating and famous people would be there. My husband was out of town and I dreaded going by myself; old terrors of not knowing anybody and not knowing what to say—how to make small talk—visions of being a wallflower again flooded me with anxiety.

I had almost decided not to go when I discovered three people I knew well had been invited. I asked exactly what time they expected to get there; in order not to be earlier, I walked around the block four times—*me*—a grown-up, successful lady of fifty-two! My friends never arrived— some emergency at their office. The host welcomed me with great warmth, but he was busy. For the next half hour I thought I would die. There were strained conversations with some people he had introduced me to; there were agonizing periods of trying to look busy, with a cigarette or a drink. I was trying to figure out how I could leave, invisibly, when I was greeted by a famous puppeteer and his wife. *They* had been fans of *my* television program! I couldn't believe it; Wendy and I had watched him on television for years—how could such a great and talented man have been interested in *me*? We all embraced like long-lost friends; the conversation was animated; we were joined by others who got interested in what we were saying. All of a sudden a number of people who were *really* famous were telling me they knew *me*! I had a wonderful time!

As I walked home, elated, stimulated, I began to sneeze; was I getting a cold? It seemed ridiculous—I'd been perfectly well until this minute. When I got home I had a consultation with myself. Often the onset of a cold occurs when there is something I want to cry about. But why should I want to cry when I'd had such fun? I began to cry—harder and harder. The sneezing stopped; no cold. *I was crying with relief.* That frightened, self-hating wall-flower of a teen-ager was finally exorcised. I had, after all, learned to be myself—and because in these recent years I had been using my talents and feeling my feelings, I had helped other people. My pleasure in myself had been contagious—for there was a common theme in those who came up to speak to me. In one way or another each said, "You are so real on television and in what you write. I always have the feeling you are inviting everyone else to be real, too."

I wish my mother had understood that—for herself as much as for me. I wish I'd understood that when my daughter was growing to womanhood. But mostly I'm so grateful to have learned—no matter how long it may have taken—*that learning to please myself has been the key to being helpful and loving to others.*

The way I feel about it now is that young people should be encouraged to develop their own experimental options. If they are scared or shy or late developers, they should be encouraged by parents and peers to respect their own natures. That should be the keystone; think about who you are and what you feel and respond accordingly, knowing ideas and feelings are always in flux and attention must be paid to one's inner messages at frequent intervals. The freedom to *reject* freedom is absolutely essential and we need to encourage and support a young person's examining his or her readiness for new experiences. For those young people who are ready to explore the unknown, who need to discover themselves sexually and to learn about interrelationships from direct experience, I think we ought to provide the guidance and counseling that would make this possible with minimal hazards. The experience of loving is surely one of the best ways in which human beings learn about synergy. What better way is there to discover that to give oneself wholeheartedly to the pleasure of loving brings joy as well to the person one loves? And how many people, caught in the fragile, poignant, heart-shattering awakenings of love, want to hurt anyone, start a fight, see other people unhappy? The gratification, the joy of loving, when it is not crippled by shame and guilt, can be the most civilizing force in the world. The same is true in all creative experiences. The artist discovers that the more genuine the personal experience he communicates on a canvas, or in a piece of music—the more pleasure he gives himself—the more he enriches others.

This is not to suggest that human beings, being human, can hope to eliminate jealousy, rivalry, unrequited love, rejection, and exploitation. And certainly the pain of loving may be greater when one is young, inexperienced, and immature. But pain is an intrinsic part of growing, and rather than constricting the adolescent's opportunities for experimentation, we ought to make it clear that genuine feelings and painful experiences can be harmful and damaging, but are not fatal. Quite the reverse—this is the beginning of greater understanding.

It seems to me the hazards of greater freedom during adolescence are a small price to pay if encouraging a quest for personal fulfillment could lead young people to truly care about each other. By stifling so much of the hidden agenda of needs, we end up with adults who enjoy watching people beat up other people; who find scapegoats as targets for their own self contempt; who are suspicious of strangers, hostile to people who are different; who devote their lives to seeing how much richer and more powerful they can be than anyone else.

If one were to take a census of which people in our current American society are most deeply committed to the ideal of cooperation—who are most ready to make necessary personal sacrifices for the good of the whole—I *know* we would find that these are the people who are always in process, always searching for the treasures within themselves.

Young people today are far less prone to sell their souls for love and security than my generation were. Many of them have been deciding on the side of their own natural propensities. But we still waste a lot of our time worrying, wondering where we failed. It seems to me that the youngster who chooses to travel, to live with families in other countries, to study meditation in India or go on an African safari to photograph what's left of our wild animals rather than do what too many are doing—sitting out four years in some college, waiting for life to happen—will have fewer regrets at forty or fifty than many of us have. Of course, there are many adolescents and young adults who, given every possible alternative, would still choose a more circumscribed blueprint and never feel they were missing anything. My concern is for those we condemn with our anger, guilt, and anxiety because to be most truly themselves they must listen to a different drummer. We ought to begin to encourage children as early as thirteen or fourteen to experiment with many alternative experiences, both in and out of school. W need to be imaginative about creating meaningful work experiences for teen-agers; it is a sad commentary on a democratic society that the only socially supported and approved alternative to advanced schooling is entry into one of the armed services. If we had the same careful planning and a genuine commitment to a Peace Corps–Vista type of program, through which any young person sixteen or over could experiment with different kinds of work experiences until he found his special niche, we'd have lots of needed social services—and ultimately a lot better doctors, lawyers, plumbers, architects, politicians, teachers, social workers.

I have been greatly concerned with the apparent political apathy of the teen-agers of the mid-seventies. Whenever I ask what they think happened, they all say the same thing. Young people are discouraged, they feel hopeless, they don't believe they can make a difference; they have given up, except for certain odd pockets of the country where political activism and genuine participation in decision making has been encouraged. I think teen-agers just reflect how we all feel. We are still reeling from the tragic quality of recent American politics—we are all paralyzed. Given opportunities involving real challenge and autonomy, I think we'd see a rapid change.

As for schooling, I would love to see clusters of learning centers in every town and city—not just for kids but for everybody. Compulsory schooling would end at sixteen. From that point on, everybody, from sixteen to a hundred and six would have an opportunity to take courses on any subject under the sun, without regard to age or previous background. What a fascinating cross-fertilization of the generations *that* could be! What joy to be a teacher in a school where everybody has chosen to learn! All learning with and from each other—a synergistic society in every school building!

I recently heard about an unusual high school graduation. Nobody wore the traditional gowns, and the students handed their diplomas *to each other* as a symbol of their love for each other. There were no individual honors bestowed. Instead the principal was asked by the student council to simply say, "This class is proud of its members who have achieved special distinction—and just as proud of those who have not." That must be quite a school! It certainly seems to represent a move in the right direction.

At the same time that I have become aware of some of the ways in which I tended to postpone some aspects of my life by retreating into safe avenues of conformity, it is equally true that there were elements in my life that still encouraged many areas of self-testing and fulfillment. My parents were busy, active people—interested in every aspect of cultural, social, political issues. Their dinner parties teemed with fascinating people—leaders in every field of endeavor—and my brother and I were almost always included in their discussions. (During the early months of our courtship, I wrote long letters to Larry describing some of the interesting social events in my home. At one point he wrote back, "If I ever get back to New York and am invited to dinner, I expect to find Mme. Chiang Kai-shek and Winston Churchill playing a duet on the piano!") As for my life at an experimental, progressive high school, it was remarkable and unique—so much so, that it made me aware of even greater possibilities for positive change. While we were still weighted down with all those incredibly *silly* requirements (why in the name of God I had to be tortured through algebra and geometry escapes me utterly) we were offered far more alternatives for self-expression and exploration. My writing abilities *were* fully appreciated; I could be in plays; I discovered that I loved sculpting in clay; student government was taken very seriously. Most of all, there was a high percentage of truly gifted, dedicated teachers in the school—attracted by the opportunity to work with smaller classes, with greater freedom to experiment. They were our friends, our role models. I sill remember them with great affection, and even though some of them taught subjects I had trouble with, like French and biology, I felt appreciated as a person, and *that* is what I remember—not the rules of grammar or the classifications of living things. What seems even more incredible in the light of most high school programs is that I was allowed to "major" in child development during the last two years.

My strong feelings about the necessity for allowing young people to explore all of their innate possibilities with greater freedom comes, therefore, not only from an awareness of feelings of frustration, but equally from feelings of gratification.

There were so many synergistic elements in my life, both at home and at school, that it made it possible for me to become greedy for more. Whatever their human limitations, almost everybody with whom I had any kind of significant relationship was struggling to become more than he or she was. I joined their striving.

Aside from home and school, there was a third major influence in my life—The Society for Ethical Culture, where I attended Sunday School and, later on, various youth groups. Here, too, I felt the searching, the struggling, the consciousness that none of us were yet all we could be.

However, it now seems to me that there was an underlying streak of puritanism, a rigid morality in much too much emphasis on being "a good person" *by helping others*. The religion I have fashioned for myself is the other way around: learn to *be good to yourself* and your relations with everyone else will inevitably become more compassionate —more ethical.

Over the platform in the meeting house of the Society, there is a statement: "The Place Where Men Meet to Seek the Highest Is Holy Ground." As a youngster I interpreted that to mean that the place where men met "to do good" was holy ground. I understand its subtler and more profound dimensions now—but I think what would be even more meaningful to me would be to change that statement to "The Place Where Men and Women Meet to Seek to Become Most Truly Themselves Is Holy Ground."

I have never met a person who really liked himself, and treasured his own life, who didn't want the very best for the rest of the human race. That to me is the essence of integration of the self and others—and that is the message we need to get across to adolescents.

In the spring of 1939, toward the end of my own adolescence and the beginning of the awful rumblings that would become World War Two, I wrote a short "composition".

> Today was spring! Suddenly the sun was whispering to the cotton puffs of clouds and snow trickled down the hill, laughing and winking up at blueness. The air smelled of small wood fires and wet lush grass,

tingling with morning. There was no fear in the day. I felt like shouting and teasing the earth to laugh with me.

This is a love kind of day. It needs long strides and hands clasped. It needs blowing hair and secret laughter. It cries out for something young and trembling. It wants two people to climb up a high hill—jumping puddles in laughter—so high that if they reach up they can catch a sun-touched cloud.

I climbed the hill alone. But I did not dare reach up. Rather, I looked down and saw a small family-kind-of town far below me. I thought of the Sunday dinners inside the white houses. I thought I heard a child laugh and there was a smell of roasting chestnuts and hot coffee. A whisper of water, the sun, a cool wind. A lazy cloud looking down at the town with me.

No one here to share the beauty. No one to want a Sunday town as I do. No one to rush with me, chasing the clouds along the river.

The sun caressed my cheek and whispered, "soon, soon.

Oh, that sweet yearning for life to begin! For all young people, everywhere, may "soon" become "now."

Chapter 5

One day, just before I began writing this book, I was having lunch with a young father and we were discussing what I planned to write about. At one point he said, quite casually, "Well, you know, of course, Eda, that today children are an impediment." I couldn't understand why the walls of that quiet, elegant restaurant didn't begin to shake and tremble. I must have looked faint, because my companion looked very surprised. When he asked me what was the matter, I told him, "What you have said so casually is an idea that is almost entirely new to the history of human civilization, and yet in the past few years it has become so ordinary that you say it without even expecting to be struck by lightning!"

Several years ago a nine-year-old friend of mine—bright and articulate and sensitive—was watching a television talk show with her mother. An author was holding forth on the joys of childlessness, how wonderful it was to be free to travel wherever and whenever she and her husband pleased, and how much freer they were to pursue their own interests without being tied to an infant's needs. After a few minutes of thoughtful listening, Liz turned to her mother and said, "That lady makes me feel guilty for being born."

For the last ten years or so, I have become increasingly frightened by what has seemed to me a turning against childhood and children. My second book, published in 1967, *The Conspiracy Against Childhood,** represented a growing feeling that in spite of appearing to be a child-centered nation, we were making childhood a more and more dangerous, difficult, and unhappy experience by pushing children too hard, creating an unhealthy environment for them to grow in, and by losing touch with our own humanity—largely determined by memories of our own childhood.

Now, looking back, that book seems ridiculously naïve; what has happened since has been far worse than I could have imagined.

Although I thought I'd done with writing about children, I found it was still a subject nagging at me; there *must* be something more I could do or say, for it seemed to me we were—are—on a suicidal course. And yet I had already

* Atheneum, New York.

written *so much* about childhood—was there anything more?

My hope is that there *must* be a way of turning the tide. When we turn away from childhood, we cut ourselves off from our own deepest needs and feelings, and we give up all hope for the future.

I hope I have written about some things about childhood that may help to reaffirm why children are important to grownups, whether they are parents or not. I believe that concern for childhood is our only chance for survival. The child in us, the children yet unborn—the human and tender hope. I persist because the alternative—to give up—is unendurable.

The greatest gift any of us ever has is this tiny life we're given, and no matter what the odds of making that life count, it seems to me that one has to keep on trying; that that is what life is all about—the search, the struggle, the faith that goes beyond rational belief, that says, "No matter how things look, it's still possible. . . ."

In the process of living one's life as fully and as honestly as one can and continuing to fight for what one believes, there are moments of exultation and joy. Those of us who love being human, vulnerable, mysterious in our possibilities still care for each other, and while we often seem to be powerless, we are not weak. So long as we have the strength and the courage to search for our own humanity and protect what is most human in others, there is still some hope for the necessary changes that must now take place.

What comforts me the most is the part of me that stays

open and vulnerable, that stays curious and alive—that *hurts* so much. It is the part that doesn't ever get old and tired and tough, the part that remains a child full of wonder and sensitivity and lovingness. When I cannot bear to read another headline, or listen to another insane government official talk the gibberish of the theater of the absurd, I turn away from being a grown-up, middle-aged woman and try to get in contact with the innocence and courage of the child in me. It is not an escape from reality, it is an affirmation of my humanhood; and when I am refreshed, I go on working for life, no matter how discouraging the situation seems.

Ultimately, personally, as adults, the meaning of childhood is that each of us has a child companion who can be with us always—to love us, amuse us, help us continue to look at the world around us in wide-eyed wonder. It is this child part of ourselves that can keep us in closest touch with what we were most truly meant to be—what makes us unique, special, beautiful beyond measure; the child is the miracle of our humanness, and the more we allow that tender part of ourselves to be a companion, the more each of our lives will truly become an extraordinary and fulfilling adventure.

Recently my husband and I visited some friends on Fire Island, at a town in which the population is largely homosexual. Shortly after our arrival we went for a walk along the beach. It came as quite a shock to discover that I began to feel uneasy, uncomfortable—even anxious. This was quite out of character for me. Could it be that in spite of my professed indifference to the technical preferences through which human beings express love for each other, there lurked a prejudice after all? Larry and I had been fighting for the rights and dignity of the homosexual community for a lot longer than most people—way before it became fashionable. We had long since rejected the psychoanalytic view that all homosexuality was merely the result of neurotic parent-child relationships, and our observations through all our professional careers had led us to the conclusion that terrible and wonderful love relationships occurred with about the same frequency among homosexuals and heterosexuals. (Have you checked the divorce rate lately?) Why then this disquiet, this apprehension?

It took me only a few minutes to figure it out. Here was a glorious beach, miles of sand, ahead and behind us, *and not a single child, anywhere.* It felt like the end of the world—some awful, unnatural, hopeless, and inhuman place, I tried to imagine what it would be like if this beach were the whole country—the whole world—and I realized in a new and deeper way than I ever had before why my life has been so preoccupied with childhood. *It is the essence of being human.*

Every time a child is born, we have another chance. The greatest miracle of all has happened; here is this mysterious and miraculous new person, with limitless possibilities for wonder and delight, tenderness and compassion, insights and gifts. Will we murder its humanity quickly, or slowly and torturously? Will we make this child glad to be alive, eager to love and be loved, or will we cripple it into a creature of self-hate and a need to destroy? Partly this will depend on whether or not this child is deeply and truly *wanted*. That is absolutely essential; parents-to-be must choose deliberately to have a child, with all careful and responsible awareness of the personal and social commitment not to continue to haphazardly overpopulate the world. The newborn child is the only real hope we have for human survival; could a time come when we could truly nurture that miracle of life in order to save all life?

But there is even more to childhood than that. What was so painful and frightening for me, on that beach, was that if there were no children, ever, anywhere, then I would lose the child in *me*. Life is a continuum, a stream, and all that we have ever been is part of what we are now, and will be. Seeing children, loving their presence in my world, watching child nature express itself, is a constant reminder of the child within, which is my humanity, my possibilities for further growing. When I am happiest, most fulfilled, most loving, there is a child being nourished in a secret garden inside of me, a child I have not forgotten to love and to cherish, until death.

That is what all species of babies are about—the miracle of miracles, the rebirth of life. And nothing in our world can help us rekindle hope as much as a human child. A baby is the ultimate antidote to human terror and despair; it is our only hope, each new baby representing the possibility of tomorrow and of something good to come.

If we want to find our way out of the crippling that has come with the overkill of technology, the exhaustion of too much rationalism, the dehumanizing of the scientific age, the way back is through childhood—our own and that of our new children. We need to recognize that a child is not an *impediment* to life but the *source* of life, and that to parent a child is to parent one's own life as well as that of one's child.

What are children for? Not to help us survive economically, not to populate the world, not to hold a family together, not to give us a sense of immortality. Children are for loving—loving what they remind us of about ourselves, loving their being most human, loving the possibilities they bring, loving the miracle of life.

If we could begin to truly garden our children; if we could give them the nourishment they need to flower most fully and beautifully; if we could help them learn to care for their own lives and thereby to care for the lives of others; if we could let go and stop trying to teach and improve, but *garden,* maybe . . . maybe . . . yes, it *is* possible. Look at the faces of the babies in a hospital nursery; watch a baby nurse; look at your own sleeping child; watch the children building a sand castle at the shore; listen to a child singing to himself in the bathtub. What do you hear? I hear a new beginning; I hear something gentle and open and alive. I hear something that is most profoundly the opposite of "made by machine." I hear something unpredictable by any tests, something mysterious. I see what is most tender in being human. I see our only hope.